The
Garland Library
of
War and Peace

The
Garland Library
of
War and Peace

Character "Bad"

The Story of a Conscientious Objector

As Told in the Letters of
Harold Studley Gray

Edited by
Kenneth Irving Brown

with a new Introduction
for the Garland Edition by
Charles Chatfield

Garland Publishing, Inc., New York & London
1971

Introduction

Character "Bad" *is the story of Harold Gray,
wrestling with himself in order to establish his
position on World War I in a series of decisions that
led him to the barracks and tents of the conscientious
objectors, to a hunger strike with Evan Thomas,
Erling Lunde, and Howard W. Moore, and at length to
prison. All of this is worked into a personal narrative
of clarity and force by Kenneth I. Brown.*[1] *It
deserves to be called a classic in the field because of
the sureness with which it communicates the public
and private experience of a man in near isolation. His*

[1] *Kenneth Irving Brown (1896-   ) graduated from the University of
Rochester in 1918, and earned his M.A. and Ph.D. degrees at Harvard
University in 1920 and 1924 respectively. After teaching biblical
literature at Stephens College (1925-30) he became president of Hiram
College (1930-40) and Denison University (1940-50). His lifelong
commitment to education for human quality and social welfare was
given great scope when he became executive director of the Danforth
Foundation, 1951-61. Under his leadership the foundation rapidly
expanded its programs and influence; and Danforth Fellows who knew
him affectionately as "Kib" can testify to the personal quality of his
leadership, the very characteristic he cherished in their teaching. His
several books on education included:* Campus Decade *(1940),* Not
Minds Alone *(1954), and* Substance and Spirit in Education *(1961).
Brown became acquainted with Harold Gray at Harvard shortly after
World War I, and even then remarked that he would like to write Gray's
story. Some years later, when he had been teaching a course on social
problems, he raised the matter again, saying that he did not know of a
good biography of a pacifist. Working with Gray's complete set of
letters to his mother, not all of which were incorporated in the book,
Brown wrote* Character "Bad."

INTRODUCTION

*letters contain searching and reflective moments; they
include a wealth of detail and a good deal of action.*
Between 1914 and 1919 Harold Gray trod an
intimate and private road upon which historians have
no inherent right to trespass. But to a large extent it
was also a part of a public travail with the meaning of
war, which it is important to record accurately and to
understand. Although many men accepted the colors
as a matter of course and although some men
objected to military service in unthinking obedience
to creedal training, other young men responded with
a series of considered decisions that pitted them
against the national war effort. The enduring value of
this book is its unusually full view of a man making
the decisions that committed him to conscientious
objection to conscription in wartime.

Gray was like a majority of his countrymen, to all
outward appearances. Born in Detroit in 1894, he was
reared in an affluent and deeply religious family. He
was very active in the Student Chrisitan Association,
both at Philips Exeter Academy and at Harvard
University. After two years at Harvard, he sailed to
England in the service of the Y.M.C.A. and its work
with Allied soldiers and German prisoners of war.

At that point his personal story gained historical
interest because he was closely associated with a
group of Y.M.C.A. secretaries who included future
influential pacifists—Kirby Page, publicist and
organizer of antiwar programs between the wars, and
Evan Thomas, chairman of the War Resisters League

6

during World War II and brother of the socialist leader Norman Thomas. Gray's letters document their experience of the war in England and their reaction to it. The close-knit group of Y.M.C.A. secretaries reviewed together the question of war in relation both to personal ethics and broad social issues. Indeed, Gray first encountered the writings of Walter Rauschenbusch in England and he was deeply influenced by them, although he had taken an active interest in religious affairs for years.

Coming upon the social gospel when they did, Gray and his friends were somewhat free from its more naïve optimism. They become suspicious of panaceas and all-purpose crusades, including the war to end war. They grounded their social concern on the value of individual freedom and they related it to the problem of suffering. Their subsequent social and religious thought was characterized by the primacy of freedom of choice, the fact of suffering, and the goal of social welfare.

The irony of the epithet "Character 'Bad' " frames the story of a man willing to undergo imprisonment for his own ideals, one who did so without a lofty sense of selfhood. "I shall oppose the state trespassing on the rights of the individual, not because I feel that the individual owes nothing to society and his fellow men, but because he owes the best he has to give," he wrote. "The last thing I want to do is to oppose my government, and I am not here to protest against the policy which they [sic] have adopted in dealing with

Germany, but only because they have ordered me to take part in something I do not and cannot believe in." [2]

He was released from prison September 5, 1919, and he returned to Harvard University, where he graduated in 1921. In the same year he married and, influenced by his wife, sailed for China where he taught economics at Central China University (Episcopal), Wuchang. He returned home in 1926 to take further work in economics at Harvard and, as he noted in the epilogue to this book, was dissuaded from returning to China because of the revolutionary turmoil there and his own growing family. Instead, he worked for a banking firm in Detroit for a while. Gray was principally responsible for the creation in 1932 of a pilot project in producers' and consumers' cooperatives, Saline Valley Farms, Michigan.

In the summer of 1963 I had the pleasure of visiting with him and his second wife, Margaret (he had remarried late in the forties), at Saline Valley Farms. I was met by a tall, somewhat angular man who carried himself erect, a man who at the age of nearly seventy was accustomed to swim over a mile a day in the very cold, spring-fed pond on the farm. Fortunately, I accepted his invitation to stay overnight, not only to see the sunset grace fruit-laden Michigan hills, but also to share the warmth of the household and the reminiscences of my host. Conversation turned to the years when Gray had worked

[2]Character "Bad", pp. 135, 175.

8

out the tenets of his convictions, to the Second World War when he reaffirmed them by publically declining to register for the draft, and to beliefs he still maintained.

The freedom of the individual person was primary in his thought, and a willingness to suffer still was regarded as a concomitant of freedom. "If you grant another freedom of choice, you may be made to suffer the consequences of an abuse of that freedom," he said.[3] "It is his freedom that makes suffering a virtue; suffering is virtuous only in relation to the cause for which one suffers, not in itself. If you believe, as I do and as Jesus taught in his life and death, that God has endowed as all with personality and freedom, that is a cause worth suffering for. I think God, like Christ on the cross, suffers when men abuse their freedom and in so doing cause others to suffer. Otherwise I have no answer to the problem of evil in the world. Certainly, God could destroy freedom by violence; that he does not is a sign of the valuation God puts on human freedom to choose.

"So, too, society may suffer from an abuse of freedom. If we are concerned with dissuading men from abusing their freedom, though, we must be sure that it is the specific abuse that is at issue and not men's right to decide a matter for themselves.

[3] This conversation is constructed from an interview with Harold Gray on August 29, 1963, from correspondence with him, and from his letter to Attorney General Francis Biddle, April 27, 1942, in Alfred Hassler, Conscripts of Conscience (New York, 1942), also reprinted in the Garland Library of War and Peace.

Otherwise, the issues are hopelessly confused between regulations that are for the social welfare and restrictions of human freedom. A lot of people who will accept the former will resist, even fight, the latter. Prohibition may serve as an example. Military conscription is a far more serious one."

Gray spoke more slowly now, linking past and present as he reached for critical distinctions. *"I am conscientiously opposed to all war, I feel so keenly that the evil consequences of a resort to violence so far outweigh any possible advantages from its use that when my country demands my war service, I am compelled to protest. My refusal to register in World War II was a necessary part of that protest because that was the point at which the wartime state cornered me. But beyond this, I am convinced that war is a denial of the God of love and forgiveness, our God who gives us freedom knowing that we will abuse it. War requisitions conscience when it requires conscription.*

"Conscription represents a claim on the part of the state for control over the life and services of citizens which I believe encroaches too far upon the rights of the individual. Such a claim springs from the image of the state as an end in itself whose authority tends to become absolute. My objection goes still deeper. For me conscription represents a dividing line between my allegiance to God and my loyalty to the state. I believe that a man's highest duty is to live up to the light as he sees it. This applies as much to the man

10

who believes in the necessity of meeting violence with violence as to the man who does not. The soldier is prepared to pay for his conviction with his life, if necessary; certainly the pacifist should be prepared to sacrifice no less.

"I lay no absolute claim to having been right in 1917-19 or in 1942, although I believe I was; but to act as if I were right was the only course open to me under the circumstances. The world goes forward when men live up to and seek to apply what they believe, honestly and fearlessly, even though history may later prove that they were mistaken. That cause for which one will suffer is what we call truth, and every man must act—and be allowed to act—according to his understanding of truth."

It is said frequently, even tritely, that consistency is the hobgoblin of little minds. A brief visit with Harold Gray, like a reading of this book, is persuasive evidence that consistency may be also the hallmark of hard-won faith.

Charles Chatfield
Wittenberg University
Springfield, Ohio

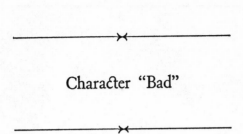

Character "Bad"

HAROLD STUDLEY GRAY

Character "Bad"

THE STORY OF
A CONSCIENTIOUS OBJECTOR

As Told in the Letters of

HAROLD STUDLEY GRAY

EDITED BY

KENNETH IRVING BROWN

HARPER & BROTHERS PUBLISHERS
New York and London
1934

*To the mother
to whom these letters were written
and to all mothers
whose sons have struggled
to find Light*

>>>>>>>>>>>>>>>>>>>>>>>><<<<<<<<<<<<<<<<<<<<<<<<

PREFACE

Character "Bad" is the story of a man trying desperately
to find his way to Truth. Because he was a man in whose
life religion was both a background and a foreground, a
compulsion and a stimulus, he thought of his goal in religious terms, calling it "the Will of God." When by
means of study, conversations with friends and trusted
advisers, long hours of prayer and deep meditation, he
came to a satisfying understanding of that Divine Will for
his life, he set himself so to live that that Purpose might
have complete control. It was a costly adventure, but he
saw it thru; in public contumely and bodily pain the
price was heavy, but he did not waver.

The solutions to the persistent evils of war and conscription which the adventurer accepted are not the solutions
popularly held; as permanent solutions they may be right
or they may be wrong. Unwritten history and events yet
to be born must prove or disprove their validity. For one
man, however, they came as answers bearing the authentic
stamp of Truth, bringing the obligation that he accept
them in theory and live them as fact. This he did to the
full measure of his intelligence and strength.

The letters are offered in excerpt as they were written
during the days of national and world upheaval, save for
the minor corrections in spelling and grammar which a
hasty second reading would have suggested. They are not

[vii]

in a literary vein; they are a young man's letters to his
family, most frequently to his mother, chatty, personal,
concerned with the week's routine, its perplexities and its
delights. There is about them the revealing intimacy of
a diary.

Altho faced with the need of crowding much into
brief space and of giving first place to those events and
influences which brought the adventurer to the position
whereby resistance to war and to the government which
was seeking to use him to further war became a religious
necessity, the editor has tried to leave enough of the personal detail to afford the reader some understanding of the
innate kindliness and the deeply affectionate nature of the
man who for conscience sake chose the solitary way.

It is hoped that this little book will be accepted not as
a tractate on pacifism but as the simple story of one man's
sincere attempt to learn and to live the Will of God in the
face of war.

There is contagion about great-hearted devotion, there
is compulsion in unreserved consecration. The task of the
editor has brought a large measure of spiritual gain.

The figure of history that has pushed its way most frequently to mind in the course of the editor's work has been
Saint Francis, he of the dusty foot and the humble heart.
One may not share his zeal for the monastic order of life,
one may not be called to follow the path he took, one may
even be forgiven for wondering at times if the world of
hatreds and strifes is ready for the gentleness and purifying
love he had within his spirit to bestow, but all of this need
not alter in the least degree the admiration, the respect, the

affection in which one holds that man of Assisi who came
so near to the heart of a suffering Christ that he bore in
his body the marks of His pain. These have been the
thoughts swirling in the editor's mind as he has worked
with joy over these letters.

Dr. Charles Clayton Morrison saw the adventurer during
his imprisonment. As a result of that visit Dr. Morrison
wrote to Mr. Gray, Harold's father, "When I left Harold
last Saturday at Leavenworth, I carried with me a feeling
of awe, a kind of instinctive testimony that I had been in
the presence of one of the noblest souls I have ever
encountered."

Perhaps it was of such as Harold Gray that Jesus said,
"Ye shall know the truth, and the truth shall make you
free."

KENNETH IRVING BROWN

Hiram, Ohio
2 January 1934

Character "Bad"

Dishonorable Discharge from the Army of the United States

TO ALL WHOM IT MAY CONCERN:

This is to Certify, That _Harold S Gray_
Private 1st Battalion Conscientious Objector
National Army is hereby **Dishonorably Discharged** from
the military service of the **United States** by reason of the sentence of a
General Court-Martial *#92 Hqs Camp Funston*
dated _November 14th 1918_

Said _Harold S Gray_ was born
in _Detroit_, in the State of _Michigan_
When enlisted he was _24_ years of age and by occupation a _Student_
He had _Brown_ eyes, _Brown_ hair, _Ruddy_ complexion, and
was _5_ feet _9½_ inches in height.

Given under my hand at _Alcatraz California_ this
_5th_ day of _Sept._, one thousand nine hundred and _Nineteen_

Jos. Garrard

Colonel. U. S. A. Retired
Commanding.

Form No. 527, A. G. O.   * Insert grade and company and regiment or corps or department; e. g., " Corporal, Company A, 1st Infantry;" "Sergeant Quartermaster Corps;" "Sergeant, First Class, Medical Department."
† Insert "Regular Army," "National Army," "National Guard," "Regular Army Reserve," or "Enlisted Reserve Corps," as the case may be.
‡ Insert number, date, and source of general court-martial order.

FIRST PAGE OF ARMY DISCHARGE HANDED TO HAROLD S. GRAY
AT ALCATRAZ, SEPTEMBER 5, 1919

Knowledge of any vocation : Student

Wounds received in service : None

Physical condition when discharged : Good

Typhoid prophylaxis completed May 18th 1918

Paratyphoid prophylaxis completed May 18th 1918

Married or single : Single

Remarks : Character "Bad".

A SECTION OF THE REVERSE PAGE OF DISCHARGE

CHAPTER I

W HEN in the course of the World War Harold
Studley Gray was summoned to appear before the
local draft board of Detroit, he wrote himself down a conscientious objector. He had come to that position during
the previous sixteen months spent in England as a
Y.M.C.A. secretary, detailed to work in the German prison
camps. The events of that experience had brought to Gray
a bitter hatred of war with all its hideous consequences,
together with a deep and abiding conviction that any resort
to violence, whether in the use of force to coerce an enemy-
nation or of conscription to control the actions of individual
citizens, was contrary to the mind of Christ. It was a conviction which entailed inescapable obligations.

Not once thruout the difficult weeks and months that
were to follow, with their examinations and reëxamina-
tions, the period in the guardhouse of Fort Riley, the
court-martial with its sentence of twenty-five years' imprisonment at hard labor, the months at Fort Leavenworth,
and the summer at Alcatraz prison—not once did he waver
in the assurance that he had found the course which for
him was, to use his own phrase, "God's will." Thruout
his letters that note of assurance runs. There were, to be
sure, numerous situations in which he was hard pressed to
apply those principles of Christian living which he held,
days calling for decisions when he was uncertain which

[1]

course of action would best interpret the truth as he saw it. During the weeks at Camp Custer and at Fort Riley he was troubled to know the precise point where he was honor-bound to resist the government which was seeking to control his actions against his best judgment and conscience, and in retrospect Harold Gray would willingly join in a discussion of the wisdom of some of those very decisions.

Under the emotional stress of camp life, surrounded by the contumely and bitterness shown by citizen and soldier to the conscientious objector, with the government feeling its way in its dealing with this obstinate and intractable group, issuing statements and then reversing them, Gray and scores of other C.O.'s had to reach decisions of major importance. Yet far beneath this turmoil and surface-strife, undergirding these perplexing decisions of the moment, sustaining, assuring, supporting, was a certainty no logic of mankind could have dislodged that the course he had chosen was, so far as his life was concerned, in accord with the purpose and the plan of the Father-Creator of all life. This was no chance happening but the fruit of a rich ancestral heritage deeply veined with religious faith and hope.

Altho this book is concerned only with a single major episode of a life which within its thirty-nine years has proved crowded and fruitful, that episode can best be understood against a background, briefly sketched, of the family culture which molded the formative years of Gray's life.

On both maternal and paternal sides there were strongly

religious influences. His grandfather Studley, a minister in the Methodist Episcopal Church, was successful in combining a deeply spiritual outlook on life with a theology and a philosophy that were uncommonly liberal for that communion and that day. His paternal grandfather, John Simpson Gray, theologically less progressive than Dr. Studley, was a pious, faithful layman belonging to that branch of the Disciple Brotherhood which refuses to countenance the use of musical instruments in their worship services.

Harold Studley Gray, the oldest of four children, was born while Mr. and Mrs. Philip Gray were living in a recedingly-aristocratic section of Detroit, on the edge of the Polish district. The home life of his boyhood was modest, cultured, rich in religious devotion. It is no accident that again and again in the letters Gray speaks, with a frankness not common in those of his age, of his love of prayer. He was educated from boyhood in spiritual things; prayer, he was taught, is as normal and as necessary as eating.

His formal schooling began at the old Trowbridge School, in a class whose membership was largely foreign. He was class orator at his commencement in 1909, choosing, prophetically, to give his first oration on the Hague Peace Tribunal. Study at the Central High School followed, but his absorption in the religious interests of the Y.M.C.A. kept him from the academic success he might have earned. In addition, he was undertaking to teach a Sunday school class at the Central Christian Church. It was inevitable, therefore, that his schoolwork should suffer. A serious attack of blood poisoning further blocked his progress. It was the December report of his third year at

[3]

high school which brought on a family conclave; he had failed in his German, and his parents were agreed that he must relieve himself of some of the extra responsibilities he had assumed.

Phillips Exeter Academy was mentioned. A member of the family had received his schooling there. The decision was made. In January, 1912, a boy of seventeen arrived at Exeter, New Hampshire, and enrolled at the Academy in the "lower middle year." It is evidence of industry and ability that Harold was able to fulfill all the requirements of Exeter and to be graduated with his class in 1914.

At Exeter Harold found his greatest enjoyment in the Student Christian Association. When he visited Northfield during the summer of 1912 and participated in his first student conference, a determination was born within him to make the Exeter Association, of which he had recently been made vice president, a still more potent influence in the lives of the Academy students. During the years when he served as vice president and later as president, the Association sponsored a well-developed program of student meetings, deputation groups, large student representations at Northfield, and numerous social service projects.

The emphasis of all student Christian association work at this time, both on the campuses and at the conference gatherings, was on personal religion: the existence and the available companionship of God, the power of prayer, the demands of clean living. The social issues, which in the decade after the war were to become the focal points of much of this work, were not generally regarded; student groups at that time had not set their teeth into the con-

[4]

troversial problems of race relations, economic justice, war and peace.

For the understanding of Gray's later convictions and his courageous application of them in the face of opposition, the religious interests thus early developed are important. When in the autumn of 1914 he matriculated at Harvard, knowledge of his successful leadership of the Exeter Association preceded him, and he was soon invited to take part in the program of Phillips Brooks House, the clearing house for the religious and social service work of the University. He was also invited to assist Dr. Albert Parker Fitch, then president of Andover Theological Seminary, with the Bible courses which were being offered in the freshmen dormitories.

The freshman college year was for Gray, as it has been for many college students, a period of reëvaluating his religious faith. The gulf between adolescence and maturity needed to be bridged; childish certainty had to give way to a more profound assurance born of the pain of hard thinking and absolute honesty. Dr. Fitch proved his wisdom as a guide in the problems of belief which Gray brought to him, and frequent were the conferences, for a dormitory mate, skilled in polemics and lacking in any faith of his own, was taking a malicious delight in storming the citadel of young Gray's religion. The circumstance was indeed a fortunate one for it brought to Gray the necessity of critical thinking and of building from the very foundations a workable faith that could stand the stress of attack as well as the strain of agreement.

No one who was in college during those early years of

the European struggle, when the United States was trying with desperation to maintain her difficult position as a neutral, will forget the restlessness of campus life. Studies paled before the possibility of military action. Life lost much of its certainty. The more adventurous of the young men were seeking service with Canadian, British or French forces. The precariousness of the future and the inner urge to be doing militated strongly against academic concentration. Harvard, like most colleges of the country, had its student regiment, and along with hundreds of others Harold Gray joined.

In the spring of 1916, when Gray was finishing his sophomore year, Ned Carter, director of the Y.M.C.A. work in India, visited the Harvard Yard. Thru his associations with Phillips Brooks House, it was arranged that Gray should take Mr. Carter into his room for the four or five days of his visit. Mr. Carter, himself a Harvard man and a former director of Phillips Brooks House, had for his immediate mission the enlistment of some fifty men to return with him to India for work under Y.M.C.A. auspices on the troopships carrying the Indians to the war fronts.

The world east of Suez had little attraction for Gray; he was aware of no special qualifications which would fit him to do the specific work for which Mr. Carter was seeking men. Nevertheless, the restless desire to "get into things" which was charging the students was in him. Work outside of America had the appeal of adventure. It was spring and examinations were ahead.

"Robert Ewing, director of the prison camp work in England, is in need of men," Mr. Carter said one day.

"What do they do?"

"It's their job to work with the German prisoners in England."

Gray was interested. The needs of the prison groups made a strong appeal to his generous, friendly spirit. After his happy experiences in Detroit, he was certain that he would enjoy working under the International Y.M.C.A. He had spent a summer in Germany and had some acquaintance with the language.

The decision to volunteer was not an impulsive one. There were numerous consultations with advising friends, letters and replies with questions raised and answered; there were periods of quiet when Gray tried to see himself with the objectiveness of the critic, and hours of prayer. When, in May, 1916, the commitment was made which was to take him from Harvard for at least one year of endeavor in England, he wrote to his mother in the language of evangelical devotion so common to his pen in those days:

"Your first letter was by far the best because it contained the consent I have so prayed for. It was followed by Father's letter Thursday. They certainly came as an answer to prayer. As I wrote Dave Porter yesterday, the whole affair seems to be a very clear call from God. For many months back I have been praying, by myself and with . . . [others] every Monday morning, regarding the situation in Europe and our part in it. We had no idea how our prayers would be answered and it never crossed my mind that God could use me directly."

After the Harvard examinations, Gray spent ten days at Northfield. Here for the first time he met Kirby Page, whose friendship he was long to cherish. When the arrangements necessary for a lengthy absence from the country had been cared for, Mr. and Mrs. Gray accompanied Harold to New York, that they might be together up to the time of the departure. It was the *New Amsterdam* that carried overseas the little group of "Y" secretaries— some of them seasoned leaders assigned to important posts in the war-countries, others, like Gray, young novices, enlisted for "foreign service" and meeting their first assignment.

Sixteen months were to pass before Harold Gray was to return to America, and then as a man burning with the conviction that war was morally wrong. Three years were to roll by before he was to reënter Harvard to complete the requirements for his degree, and then as a student shadowed by a prison record—a prison record acquired for conscience' sake.

CHAPTER II

THE small group of Y.M.C.A. secretaries that sailed for England aboard the *New Amsterdam* on July 11, 1916, included several men who were to influence in a permanent way the thinking and consequently the life of Harold Gray. For Sherwood Eddy he had long had a warm affection, born of associations with the student conference work. Kirby Page, whose acquaintance he had recently made at Northfield, was a man nearer his own age; Mr. Page shared with Gray a zeal for "personal religion," but already he was grappling with the major social issues of our time, and his thinking on the problem of war had its effect on Harold's approach, first, to the theoretical question of Christianity and the use of force, and second, to the essentially practical question that was to arise later when America had taken her place in the alignment of the nations, what should be his action in the face of the draft-call?

A third man in the group with whom a deep friendship developed was Max Yergan, a young Negro who had already begun the building of an excellent work among his own people, a work which in the years after the war was to be continued in Africa. Yergan's happy combination of the mystic and the toiler strongly attracted Gray, as his letters show. Ned Carter, whose visit to Harvard was responsible for Harold's presence on the steamer, was also on board.

On board the *New Amsterdam*
July 19, 1916

Altho the voyage has been an uneventful one, my association with our men and the wonderful talks I have had give me so much to write about I hardly know where to begin.

Tuesday evening before dinner we all met together for prayers and we have been meeting every evening since for the same purpose. Wednesday noon we had our first meeting to talk over the work we are going to do. This meeting, too, has been held every day since, just at noon. The fellowship and spirit of these two meetings each day in itself has been worth the trip. . . .

I wish I had time to tell about each of the eight men I am with, but it would take too long. I have had wonderful talks with all of them, particularly Max Yergan and Kirby Page, my roommate.

The first letter written to his mother after his arrival in England was from London.

July 30

About six our train pulled out for London. England is perfectly beautiful and it was after ten o'clock before it got too dark to see the country from the car window.

In the compartment with me were Eddy, Page, and

Yergan. After it got dark, we pulled down the shades and had prayers. I shall never forget that little meeting. One thing this trip has taught me so far is how to pray. I say *has taught me*; I mean has started to teach me.

.Altho it was for service in the German prison camps of England that Gray had interrupted his college course and crossed the Atlantic, there were obstacles in the way of his entering upon this work at once, the greatest being the delay in procuring the necessary government passes.

No one was allowed within the prison areas with their protection of barbed wire and sentries unless approved by the British War Office, and the typical bureaucratic delay ensued. The weeks of waiting were, however, weeks of conscientious endeavor. There was need that he familiarize himself with the work that was being done among the German prisoners, and that he take charge of some of the office routine of caring for these details. The prison secretaries had used with success the idea of recreational boxes, each with a different content, to be passed from camp to camp. It fell to Gray to provide these boxes and their equipment and to arrange for their schedule of movements. In addition he was busying himself with the work of the office, delighting to bring something of American efficiency where, to his mind, it was needed.

July 30, cont.

Yesterday I got busy cleaning up the office and a worse

mess I seldom have seen. Of course they are short of help and the result is disorder and confusion everywhere. At noon I took dinner with Yergan . . . at the old Cheshire Cheese, the famous resort of Samuel Johnson. . . .

Yesterday evening Max and I heard a very fine production of *Faust*. All the theaters here are running full swing for the benefit of the soldiers on leave.

Aug. 6

I am very happy and things are going nicely. Mr. Ewing has put me very largely in charge of the office here with a regular live stenographer all my own and all the other things that go to make up an office. My office is on the top floor of the George Williams House, quite a large cheerful room.

Every morning my first duty is to sort and open the mail. There is always a number of letters of enquiry asking if we can help in tracing missing men or see why some one does not hear from friend or relative in some camp. Then there are continual orders for books to be sent to the different camps. Sometimes we have these books in stock and sometimes I have to go out and buy them, pack them myself, and take them down to the post office, and actually see them off. If I did not, they would never get away.

This week I plan to take up another kind of work in addition to my regular office work. Two nights a week I shall turn out about 12 P.M. and with the help of a machine go forth to gather in all the stray Tommies I can find and take them to the various Y.M.C.A. huts for the night. About 3 A.M. after collecting the Tommies, we go to the railroad stations and meet the incoming troop trains and help take the men to the "Y" huts or wherever else they wish to go. From then on until after daybreak it is a case of serving the troops in any capacity possible.

I suppose you would be interested to know where and how I am situated regarding quarters. Well, in my wildest dreams I never could have hoped to find a nicer place. The Esmond Hotel is situated next door to the British Museum in what was once the aristocratic part of town and is still delightfully pleasant. The hotel or, much better, boarding house is run by a convert of Moody's who has been an active Christian for many years. The hotel seems to be the stopping place for religious people, particularly "Y" men who are here for a day or two. It is the most homelike place imaginable with the nicest little housekeeper and bully meals.

I have been spending my evenings for the past week reading in the garden at the back of the house. It stays light till nearly ten. I have just reread my favorite book, *The Right to Believe* by Eleanor Harris Rowland, and today I began on a new one, *Modern Discipleship* by Woods.

Aug. 16

After breakfast I go up to my room and read a chapter out of my Weymouth Testament and then have a little quiet talk with God. My, what a difference it makes in the day's work. It surely is the best investment of time I have ever made.

Once in a while I think of the people back in America who used the word *sacrifice* in speaking of my coming to England. Sacrifice! I'd like to know who is doing the sacrificing. Of course if you use the word to mean giving up something inferior for something superior, I may have done some sacrificing, but in any other meaning the word has no place in my experience.

I think I never before realized what sin really is. Something is most assuredly wrong with the world and as I see things in a new light I want to tell you America is no exception. One of the greatest troubles, too, is with most of the so-called Christians who are content to leave things as they are because to do otherwise means uphill work. But believe me, if people refuse to pay the price to do the thing as God would have them, they will be forced to pay an infinitely higher price to do it their own way. When people refuse God's invitation to save others, they seem to have to pay a higher price to save themselves.

Well, I have gotten away from my story. If I digress now and then, you must forgive me. I am thinking about these things so much I seemingly can't help writing them down now and then.

Sunday I dined with Mr. and Mrs. Ewing in their new home in Golders Green, a suburb of London. It was the first time I have been in a home and it surely did seem nice. If God ever grants me a wife and home, I want to entertain a lot, not the nice people who can pay it back, so to speak, but the clerks and shop girls, the kind of people who find the cities "so full of people yet so devoid of companionship."

Monday night Mr. Eddy and Kirby returned to London and it sure did seem good to see them. They have been having some wonderful experiences. Yesterday Mr. Ewing granted me leave of absence until Monday so that I could go with Mr. Eddy while he works among the Canadian troops "somewhere in England." The men everywhere are as open as sunshine and we have little trouble in talking religion.

Gray's letters from England tell but half the story of his life during these months. The knowledge that all outgoing mail was strictly censored, together with the recognition that any discussion of the war-state of England might militate against his chances of working among the German prisoners, was sufficient to cause him to be discreetly cautious in his writing. It may be questioned, however, if weekly letters ever do tell more than half the story, for in their concern for items of news and matters of immediate importance, they almost invariably lose sight of the more gradual movements of thought and of life which like the tides of the sea are unnoticed except in retrospect.

Among the first to join the Harvard regiment in 1914 had been Harold Gray. In his thinking at that time Christianity and war-service presented no irreconcilable antagonisms. But first-hand acquaintance with a country at war brought its full measure of shock. One sees in the letters the recoil of a young man of twenty-two from the cruelty and the travesty on justice, the bestiality and the inhumanity which appear to be inextricably woven into the fabric of that system we call war.

War-England, so different from peace-England, must have made many of the thoughtful pause and wonder. Gray was seeing a mighty country gripped by a war-psychology that caused the crowds to roar with delight when a German Zeppelin, hit by one of the anti-aircraft guns, fell in flames, carrying to death its crew of thirty men. He was hearing England, beside herself with fear at the air raids, crying that German cities must be bombed, that German mothers and children must be killed for the English women and children who had suffered.

There was another influence potent in his thinking. He was seeing London beset with the immorality which invariably accompanies war, and the shock was of great moment. Accompanying Mr. Eddy on his trips to the training camps and spending nights on London streets caring for lonely Tommies brought to Gray a familiarity with conditions raw and primeval. The officers he met were speaking in confidence of the hideous ravages of venereal disease among their men. There were the soldiers on leave, the overseas men whose homes were far away, landing in London for their brief furloughs, woman-mad; there were the night-lines around Trafalgar Square. Life was cheap; morals were made for peace-times.

These were not impressions to be written in home letters, but deeply etched they were, nevertheless, on a sensitive spirit. Among his group of young friends, devout and determined Christians, there were those increasingly troubled by their inability to reconcile war and its consequences with the Mind of the Master. Doggedly, persistently they were doing their best to think their way thru, refusing to allow others to be their brains.

Gray was one with this small group. Here was war with its professed high ideals, and here were the hideous by-products, the gruesome side shows. He was asking a searching question which another before him had asked, Do men gather grapes of thorns or figs of thistles?

August 26

On the 15th of August Mr. Eddy and Kirby Page came to London for a day or two and took me down with them to Folkestone, the training center of the Canadian troops.

Every night that we were in Folkestone, Mr. Eddy visited a different hut, preaching sometimes to as many as a thousand men a night. He has a marvelous message for the men, and I have never known a man to grip people as he does. Kirby and I would mix with the soldiers at the rear of the crowd, and while Eddy was speaking we would keep our eyes peeled for any men whom we felt we could help after the meeting; invariably we would spot some man who had come to scoff and remained to pray. Time and again we found we could be of tremendous help to these men after the meeting was over by getting them apart and having a talk with them. The men are remarkably open, and the gospel of Christ seems to be the only thing which will satisfy their needs.

Mr. Eddy and I gained admission early in our visit to Folkestone to one of the large hospitals where we went several times to talk with the soldiers. Believe me, after talking with some of these men, the war begins to come pretty close home.

Last night we went to see the moving pictures of the battle of the Somme. War is certainly hell. It damns men's souls.

The old passage from John 3:16 is coming to have a new power over me. The thought that God "so loved the world" that He was willing to give us Christ and let him suffer and die for our sins, is beginning to make me wonder how much I love the world, and how much I am willing to do to try and further Christ's Kingdom.

September 17

It is Sunday morning and very quiet. I am writing at a little table by the window of my room on the fourth floor.

A typical day here runs something like this. I am called for my bath, a cold one, at quarter past seven; after my bath I go thru about fifteen minutes of exercises and then shave and dress. That usually takes to about eight o'clock. From then until breakfast at eight-thirty I have my quiet devotional period, the half hour in the day which has come to mean so much to me. Since arriving in England, by reading a chapter a day in my Weymouth Testament, I have nearly finished the four Gospels.

At eight-thirty I have breakfast, one of the regular English kind, with the exception of tea or coffee which I do not take. There is a big dish of oatmeal, bacon and eggs, toast and marmalade. It is the same every morning, but trust me, it is good.

CHARACTER "BAD"

Soon after breakfast I step around the corner to the George Williams House where my work for the day begins. It would be hard to describe all the things I have to do. Much of it would seem like the work of a glorified office boy, but it is absolutely necessary. Much of the time of all the secretaries, including Mr. Ewing, is necessarily taken up with apparently trivial and insignificant work.

In the evening I regularly read unless there is some one of the "Y" men staying here at the hotel, in which case we usually talk or go out somewhere.

Many of Gray's days followed the general pattern outlined in the last letter, their importance consisting in the numerous items of unimportance. Occasionally of an evening he left his books for a trip to the theater or more frequently to the opera, of which he was specially fond. Perhaps the most memorable of these evenings was the one when he attended the last performance of Forbes-Robertson's *The Passing of the Third Floor Back,* before that great actor's retirement.

At one time the letters speak of his attention to drawing up house-plans for a proposed new home. A natural skill with his hands made the occupation enjoyable and since the work he proposed to do among the German prisoners militated against his making many new English friends, doubtless the hours over the drafting board did much to relieve his loneliness and homesickness.

Mention of his first visit to a prison camp comes in the letter of September 17th. Late in August the permission

[19]

arrived to visit Frith Hill, a temporary prison camp, for four hours each week; it was not until the following February, however, that the passes to the other prison camps were issued.

Frith Hill in the south of England was a prison tent-colony designed for emergency occupation during the summer months while the more durable encampment at Blandford was in process of building. It was not until November that the transfer of prisoners to the winter camp was effected. Frith Hill was not built to withstand the heavy fall rains and with its inadequate drainage it gathered and held the waters until it became a veritable mud hole. In one of the letters Gray writes of wading ankle-deep thru mud and water as he went among the tents of the camp.

Gray's responsibility for the Y.M.C.A. work at Frith Hill was that of supplying the needs of the individual prisoners, so far as they could be supplied. In addition, on several occasions he gave illustrated lectures. He did not succeed in establishing at Frith Hill the Bible study groups which later he was to bring to other prison camps.

September 17, cont.

Three weeks ago I made my first visit to a camp. I have been going every week since. I find it impossible to spend more than four hours a week at visiting altho it may possibly be arranged so that I can spend more time later. Last week Mr. Ewing went with me on my visit. It was in the evening and I spoke to the men for a few minutes and then Mr. Ewing gave a lantern lecture on "Natural

Scenery in America." It was the first lecture they had had
in the camp and they surely enjoyed it.

It looks now as if I should have to do a good bit of
religious teaching this winter with all the difficulties such
work involves. The work on the whole is different from
what either you or I supposed when I left.

At the student conference at Swanwick which Gray had
attended soon after landing in England, he had met a girl,
the daughter of a collier, who was an ardent young socialist. Agnostic in her point of view, she had had little
sympathy for the Christianity which he had preached to
her; nevertheless, a friendship, pleasant to both of them,
had come. In this letter to his mother, he refers to one of
May's letters.

September 17, cont.

Let me quote a sentence or two from her letter. "Miss
Brown and I talked of you and I said to her 'I should have
greater hopes of Harold Gray if he were not a Christian,
but as it is, he is so busy giving out tracts and milk and
eggs, that he cannot find time to study how to prevent
human beings being used in industry in such a way that
they are reduced to being fit for nothing more than tracts
and milk and eggs'—please, I don't mean this quite
literally."

You laugh; so do I, but what a great person to work
with. Perhaps some day she will learn that I too find society not all that could be desired, that the cripples and

broken wrecks that I am daily seeing on the streets are
beginning to make an impress which with God's help may
some day add one more to the little band of Christians who
are burning to see wrongs righted instead of accepting all
that God gives and then settling back and taking it easy.
I know it costs. It cost Jesus his life, but believe me it was
worth while.

I wish I could put in writing what I feel. I think I can
say with Lord Tennyson, "You could sooner convince me
that my right hand doesn't exist than that God doesn't
exist." In the presence of Christ I know.

The words of an old hymn seem to hound me:

"I gave my life for thee;
What hast thou given for me?"

Yesterday I brought home a large recruiting poster. It
was a picture of Lord Roberts with these words: "He did
his duty. Are you doing yours?" But a greater army than
Kitchener's needs men now and needs them, God alone
knows, how badly.

October 8

I am not going to write a long letter this time; just a
few lines to let you know how much I love you all, think
of you, and pray for you. You would think after having
been away from home so much that it would come to
mean less to me, but I guess that is never the way with
really great things. The consciousness of what my home
has meant and does mean seems only to be dawning upon
me. I wish I could put in writing some of the things I
feel. God has been so good to me. Over here I am begin-

ning to see things perhaps not altogether differently, but certainly with greater clearness. How much in need the world is! I love to think of you every day back home doing your bit to minister to this need.

Last Wednesday on a few hours' notice I got seventy-two slides of New York and in the evening without any preparation except what I was able to get on the train, gave a lecture on New York before an audience of several hundred.

I am very busy, on the go from early till late. I seem to be in the best of health altho I am not getting quite as much exercise as I should like. Consequently I am getting a bicycle, both for my work and pleasure.

The experiences which were coming to Gray, both in London and at Frith Hill, were nurturing the doubts earlier aroused; his reading, almost exclusively devotional in nature, was strengthening his reliance on a spiritual God for guidance and there was being born in his soul a conviction that war was not the method by which the Kingdom of God was to be established. The first tentative statement of this judgment comes in a letter to his mother dated October 22, 1916.

October 22

. . . Kirby and I have been trying to thrash out the problem of whether a man is ever justified in using force to the extent of taking life, particularly in the light of Jesus' life and teachings. I must confess, tho the news may

[23]

cause you to doubt the soundness of my upper story, that in view of this world situation with all its countless by-products, I am convinced we have fallen far short of grasping the teachings of Jesus. My admiration for the conscientious objector is growing.

November 13

I also rejoice to see Wilson has been elected. Any man who will keep America out of this war deserves to be decorated. . . . I am a pacifist from the word go, if you mean by that one who is opposed to war under all conditions. I am not a pacifist in the sense that I believe in doing nothing. The only way to overcome evil is by good— aggressive goodwill. If you can love a man and at the same time kill him, all right. I don't think I could. Naturally I am keeping pretty quiet over here. It is not the place to air one's views; but I can't help having them all the same.

November 26

I spent last Wednesday and Thursday with the men at the new camp at Blandford.[1] We are planning a large $2500 hut which we are to build ourselves. I expect to get special privileges during its erection which will enable me to supervise its construction as well as afford me a splendid chance for definite Christian service. I have some wonderful men to work with. The commandant was most kindly disposed towards our work in the old camp; he is even

[1] This was the winter quarters for the men from Frith Hill.

more so now in the new. He is a man with a great big heart, able to see above petty prejudices and hatreds.

I usually spend from eight to ten hours on the train every time I go to Blandford. The time before last we were just leaving Waterloo Station, London, when one of the guards and a young girl helped another young girl into my compartment. She was evidently poor as she was very lightly clad and shivering with the cold. Fortunately I had my fur coat with me as well as a heavy sweater. I put the sweater on myself and the coat on her. I guess she would have frozen if I had not. As it was I had to get off the train before she did and take my coat from her. I had a guilty conscience about it and now wish I had gone on with her.

The same trip on the return journey I found myself in a compartment with six soldiers and a mother with a six weeks' old baby. She had been traveling all day with it and her arm was nearly broken. It has been a good while since I have held a baby but I volunteered, and the poor mother gladly accepted my offer. For over two hours I held the wee little thing and when we arrived in London about midnight I got a taxi and took them to their home.

December 6

I suppose it is hard for you at home to realize that even in a warring nation things can become routine. But such is the case. With the exception of a weekly visit to my camp and the opera, one day is much the same as all the rest. My work doesn't bring me in contact with many persons, which may be for the best. In view of my work I am not overly keen to meet people. It is not always easy especially in America to understand the feeling here.

The popular feeling which Gray refers to was a part of the war-psychosis. There was a natural expectancy that an able-bodied man, British or otherwise, would find his place in the army, and a resentment against consideration of any kind being shown to the German prisoners. Work in the prison camps was probably the least popular, publicly, of all the Y.M.C.A.'s endeavors.

December 26

Monday's mail brought a letter from the War Office granting us permission to publish a little booklet of Christmas carols as our present to all the prisoners in England. We had prepared the book over a month before and had run off a few sample copies when it became necessary to get permission to circulate it, which naturally we sought before printing. Copies were taken personally to the War Office and there the matter rested until last Monday. We had given up all hopes of permission arriving before Christmas and had practically canceled our order when the permission came. By forced shifts the printer succeeded in getting it to us in time, but, believe me, we had to do some hustling to get it into the camps.

A letter to Dr. John R. Mott, dated January 1, 1917, gives a survey of the work of the previous six months and of

Gray's activities in the prison camps of Frith Hill and Blandford.

January 1

The Christmas season is over and I am back again from Blandford where I spent my holidays. Blandford is a picturesque little town and altho I was alone in a deserted little hotel, I spent a profitable and happy Christmas there. For one thing it enabled me to clear up some letters which have been hanging over me for some time and for another it made possible my spending Christmas evening in a German prison camp.

It was a unique experience to say the least, this Christmas away from home within the barbed wire, but before describing the occasion I want to go back and tell how I came to make the acquaintance of these men, many of whom are now like old friends.

My work as secretary here began the first of August and towards the close of the month I received my pass to visit a camp of naval prisoners situated at Frith Hill. On the last day of August, therefore, with a heartbeat slightly above the normal I passed the first sentry and faced the commandant at Frith Hill.

He was a large man with a neck like a bulldog's and a stern official bearing. He was standing with two other officers as I stepped up, and for once I almost wished the ground would open up and take me in, but my judgment of the colonel was certainly incorrect for as soon as the ice was broken, I found beneath the official exterior a heart as big as a barn. He informed me that while he did not in

[27]

any way want to pamper the men entrusted to his charge, he did want to see everything reasonable done for them.

After tea with the officers, I was turned over to the interpreter, a young Cambridge man with a heart like his chief's, who proceeded to take me past two more sentries within the third hedge of barbed wire and into the camp. I almost hesitate to say I was surprised. I have since vainly tried to recall what I expected to find within this area, in extent scarcely larger than a good-sized city block. Yet this much is sure. I did not expect the clean-cut smiling faces which greeted me.

There were several university men there who spoke English fluently and who certainly did not correspond to the current idea of savage Huns. Conversation with these men was not difficult. After a short meeting with the camp leaders, I had the pleasure of watching an intensely interesting game of fist-ball. It was no scrub-game either, as we should say in America. The sides had been well chosen and practiced and they played with skill. The spectators cheered the plays and seemed for the time to have forgotten their servitude altogether.

On my return to London I at once sent out a large marquee with tables, chairs and benches to form a recreation center, the only one in the camp. A piano soon followed and then a large lantern for illustrated lectures.

It was well into September before I began to try my skill as a lecturer. I shall never forget the first night. The tent, while of a fair size, was never built to accommodate the whole camp, and the men were packed in like sardines with a fringe six deep all the way round the outside. It was with the greatest difficulty that the interpreter and I succeeded in worming our way into the tent. The seventy-two slides of "A Trip Round the World" were some I had picked up in London. My knowledge of German, never anything to boast of, has suffered much since I studied it and would not allow me to lecture in anything but English, which proved well, as I was aided by a splendid German interpreter. The men rather prefer that I lecture this way as it gives them a chance to hear English.

Before the camp was broken up and finally moved into winter quarters, I had the opportunity of delivering four lectures altogether, one on a "Trip Round the World," one on "The States," one on "Modern New York," and one on "Modern Art," as well as providing the slides for several other lectures which various men in the camp were able to give themselves.

Early in November the whole camp was moved to its present quarters here at Blandford. The men did not bring the Y.M.C.A. tent as the commandant has kindly consented to let them use a large dining hall as a theater, and the American Y.M.C.A. has appropriated $2,500 for a fine hut, the building of which it will soon be my privilege to supervise, altho the work will be done entirely by the men.

For the past month the men have been busy erecting a stage at our expense in the large dining hall and there has been no end of preparations for a play which had its opening performance on Christmas night. It was this play towards which the camp and myself alike had eagerly looked forward for over a month.

The camp at Blandford is some distance from the town

and it is necessary to make the trip each time by motor. On Christmas evening when I started out from Blandford in the machine, it was pitch black as every street lamp for months has been out of service and the windows of those houses, where there were lights, were heavily curtained. For a time we sped along in the dark, without headlights, scarcely able to see more than a few yards away. Then suddenly as we rounded a corner we caught sight of a brightly lighted area, which, from the distance, struck one as being the most cheerful spot in England. As the machine came to a halt outside the camp, however, this impression faded. There were yards and yards of tangled barbed wire, and now and again we caught the flash of a bayonet as a sentry would wheel about to traverse again his little platform high up in the air.

When I arrived, the officers had already entered the camp; after a short wait two figures came hastening to the gate, one an English officer to give to the sentry the password which should admit me, and the other a smiling German whose first words, after the great iron gate had been swung open enough to permit my entrance, were "Merry Christmas" spoken in good English.

The crowd had assembled when I arrived, and I found them in a hall about a hundred feet by thirty feet, seated facing a firmly built stage complete in every detail. To the right of the stage was a large Christmas tree, its candles burnt low after the celebration of the previous evening. On the left was an orchestra composed of twelve musicians with their music stands built from scraps of wood left over from the stage.

The play, entitled *Fräulein Vokter*, was a little comedy of four acts. The infinite pains expended for weeks past in its preparation were not without effect. Naturally funny, this little play in the hands of these men became the cause of peal after peal of unchecked laughter from the assembled crowd.

The periods between acts were filled by music from the orchestra, music of a splendid character thru which the audience sat in complete silence. When the performance was over, the men lined up on either side of the central aisle while the officers and I made our exit. As we passed there was a smile on nearly every face, and I felt repaid for any trouble this event had occasioned me. For these men the hardship of another Christmas away from home and in prison had been made more bearable.

January 11

Monday night I sat up till late reading *Prussianism and Its Destruction* and found it of the greatest interest. I was reading it in preparation for a seminar which was held at Mr. Ewing's on Tuesday night. Some time ago we seven American secretaries agreed to read five hundred pages per month on some topic in connection with the present war. Each man further volunteered to lead the discussion of this reading at one of seven meetings to be held thruout the winter, one each month.

The meeting Tuesday night, led by a man named Evan Thomas, was on the topic of the individual's relation to the state and centered largely around the position of the conscientious objector. In April or May it will be my voluntary duty to defend this individual and the position of the pacifist generally. I shall have to do no end of reading in preparation, as well as write a paper on the subject. I am not the only man in the crowd that believes war is wrong, altho naturally outside of our little clique I am keeping pretty mum.

January 28

Spiritually I am getting rusty. Instead of coming in contact with others and setting them on fire and thereby keeping myself aglow, I seem to be burning lower and lower. I believe there is a certain point spiritually to which a man can rise by merely receiving but beyond which it is absolutely impossible to go until he begins to give. My giving seems to have stopped and I have gone as far as I can go without it.

The nature of my work makes the circle of friends and those among whom I move very small. This may be hard to understand but it is exactly the same experience which others have found to be true in this work. It is hard for people to see a husky young man of military age minus khaki without wanting to know why, if they have the least provocation for asking. If you have a good imagination you can fill in the rest.

Meanwhile there were clarifying and maturing in Gray's mind convictions regarding war and the social implications of the Christianity he was attempting to live. His work each day brought food for reflection and, on Sunday, Dr.

Orchard's meaty sermons were proving both disturbing and reassuring—disturbing to the even tenor of his ways and reassuring in his eager seeking for fuller understanding, for light in darkness.

February 11

On Friday, February second, the long awaited passes at last arrived, three of them for three of the finest camps in England, Dorchester, Blandford, and Pattishall, together containing close on to ten thousand men.

Sunday morning, February fourth, I came down to breakfast to learn from my English friends that it was all over, that the long deferred break between the States and Germany had at last occurred. The news came like a blow for which I was not prepared. My mind naturally began to contemplate what effect this would have on our work, especially in Germany. Altho a week has passed we have heard nothing. What may happen we do not know. For the present everything is going smoothly with us. We anticipate no interference and you may be sure we will stand by the job until we are forced to leave.

All during the past week we have heard reports of preparations for war in America. I dread to think of her entering this hell. For my part I am a conscientious objector from the word go. They may shoot me if they like, but they won't make me fight. Of course I don't expect such a necessity but that doesn't alter the facts.

Tuesday last week I set out for Blandford. When I arrived there, I found some sickness and on the advice of the commandant I did not enter. The government instead of permitting us to build a hut has kindly consented to appropriate a hut now there for our use and we are planning to fit it up nicely with partitions making class rooms, etc.

For the past two weeks I have worked almost incessantly at my German. Considering the time expended the result, as usual, is very poor. With the prospect in sight of possibly conducting religious services in German, you can see that I am not studying it for pleasure alone.

I forgot to mention earlier that I went this morning to hear the great pacifist, Dr. Orchard, and listened to the greatest peace sermon I have ever heard. After the service I went up to shake Dr. Orchard's hand. When he learned of my work he invited me out to dinner and we had a most interesting talk. He is a man who certainly stimulates thought.

February 18

Altho the address at the head of this letter is that of our office, I am writing in my little room at the Esmond. It is mine still altho I fear another week must find me in other quarters. My days at the Esmond are numbered and whether I will or no I must seek quarters elsewhere.

The state of public opinion is a hard thing either to describe or define, and the task is in no way made easier when one must weigh one's words with care. It has been two weeks now since the crisis between our nation and Germany came to a head in the breaking off of diplomatic relations. With that break something happened in Germany, no one here knows just what, and the first thing we knew there was a newspaper report that our men (I mean Y.M.C.A. men) had left the country. With the withdrawal of our men from Germany, everyone here seems to have taken it as a matter of course that we would abandon our work among the German prisoners. This, of course, from a Christian point of view we are totally unwilling to do until compelled to by the government, but we thereby become open apparently to the charge of being pro-German, a charge which, I can assure you, is anything but true. While the treatment of their prisoners by the British is admirable, there is little love lost for them by the general public, and anyone who attempts in any way to minister to them even if only in a spiritual way is not only open to suspicion but he finds his lot generally a rather uncomfortable one.

The above fact is not new; I have written about it before. I have also written to the effect that I have done some tall thinking about war in general and reached for my personal guidance at least some conclusions which, however, at this time and under the present circumstances it is the better part of wisdom to keep still about. But there are times when one's very silence or faint praise condemns one more than the most rabid sermons might and the occasions when this is possible, seek to avoid them as one may, are numerous.

Moreover I am an American and while the English press may at times praise my nation, it must at least be said that in general American stock is not above par. There is no doubt in their minds that we are a nation of cowards, whose moral sense is dead (or we should have been in this war of righteousness long ago) and whose only occupation is a mad scramble after the almighty dollar.

So much for a background. I have made several friends at the Esmond, people principally in religious or Christian work, and as an almost inevitable result they have learned of my work, and while with only a few have I found sympathy, I have at least found toleration. Last week I was away Wednesday and Thursday as usual visiting two of my camps. On Friday morning at breakfast without my having raised the subject one of the men who is interested in the work began to question me about my trip, and I answered him as briefly and as simply as I could. As I was about to leave for the office, the housekeeper came up to me and in a sort of joking way said she wished I wouldn't talk so much about the Germans especially at the table as all the guests were asking whether I was not a German or at least pro-German, and then putting all jesting aside she said people were doing a good deal of talking and I had better keep still about my work.

I had a long talk with the manager, and while he sympathized with my position it was clear to see that he would be glad to get rid of me. My presence is almost a stigma.

Tuesday was the day on which our committee met and in the afternoon we adjourned to Mr. Ewing's to hear a very interesting paper on Treitschke's influence upon modern German thought by one of our number. The paper itself was excellent; it was followed by an interesting discussion after which we had another of those delicious standing lunches.

This morning I went again to hear Dr. Orchard. You

have no idea how refreshing it is for one like myself undergoing as I am some revolutionary changes of thought to hear a man who is totally dissatisfied with things as he finds them and who has courage enough to say so in the very face of imprisonment.

Since beginning this letter I have been out for a walk and incidentally located what promises to be a very nice little room in a large hotel where I can lose myself in the crowd. For the present, at least, I must seek my friends only among my colleagues and the men in the camps. In spite of all the apparent hardships, this work has many, many redeeming features and I almost dread to think of giving it up.

February 25

If you will try the impossible task of picturing yourself a man within an area perhaps about the size of four good-sized city blocks, beyond which tho you possessed complete health you could not go, with nothing but men around you day in and day out, far from those you love and ever anxious about their welfare, with lots and lots of idle time on your hands and with almost no mental resources within yourself, with practically the only topic of conversation the war, the most depressing that has ever blackened the pages of history, daily hoping against hope that tomorrow will bring peace and put an end to this apparently interminable confinement, I say if you will try this impossible task you will have pictured the men with whom I am dealing. It is a man's job which at times almost seems impossible. I never realized how shallow my life was before. In the face of what these men must endure the little that I have to give them seems so dreadfully small I almost hang my head in shame. I think I understand better now why Christ had to suffer so much to be the world's saviour. If only these men had suffered as much in the interests of the kingdom of love as they have suffered and still are suffering for war!

March 25

Monday on my visit to Pattishall I cut quite a figure. With a big strap I fastened Father's little black bag over my shoulders. In it were three and a half dozen oranges and fifteen pounds of nails. In my hand were some ten dollars' worth of petticoats, curtains, and yards upon yards of colored cloth. Needless to say I was welcomed at the camp.

Wednesday at Dorchester I had a big package of games for the hospital, which I hung from my shoulder by the same strap, and then on my way up to the camp with the center of the town still to pass thru I bought ninety-six great big oranges which could barely be contained in three immense bags. By much stretching I was able to encompass these bags with my arms and with the right hand to hold two fingers of my left. Thus with a heavy box dangling at my hip I proudly marched thru the streets to the amusement of passers-by. How I love to shock these English!

Later when I was distributing some of those oranges among the men in the hospital one of the men as spokesman for the rest told me how much they were appreciated.

He said all the men look forward the whole week to Wednesday and if you could see their faces when I come in you could quite believe it. The Y.M.C.A. secretary there says about three o'clock in the afternoon the men begin to look at their watches and speculate on just when I shall arrive. It is wonderful to serve these men, over one hundred of them. Many of them are terribly wounded and last Wednesday they buried one with whom I had spoken on two former occasions.

I suppose things are pretty exciting in America; over here things are as cool as can be so that it is doubtlessly very difficult to tell what is going on. If war comes and the men of Harvard leave in any great numbers as they are pretty sure to do, I shan't consider coming home till the war is over. This work is far too interesting and its needs and challenges too great.

If the government recalls me, I shall first of all make every effort to get into the Y.M.C.A. work among our own men or out in Mesopotamia with the English, or failing that, I shall go into the Red Cross. I'd just as leave be shot at as a stretcher-bearer but I would rather go to prison than be shot at as a soldier.

Gray's report to Dr. Mott, dated March 18, 1917, summarizes his prison camp activities for the early months of that year. This vivid picture of the life of the German prisoner shows Gray too busily engaged to be brooding over his own personal concerns; nevertheless, here he was in almost daily contact with a by-product of a system—a

[39]

by-product and a system raising more problems than they solved. And in the face of their easy acceptance by Christian nations and Christian peoples Gray was becoming increasingly thoughtful.

March 18

Perhaps the best way to give an account of my work here among German prisoners during the past month and a half would be to give you the details of a typical week.

Monday early I leave for Blisworth, a station some three hours journey out of the great metropolis from whence I have an hour walk across very attractive country to the camp at Pattishall. My visit there usually begins with a brief chat with the commandant or the adjutant, after which I go into the camp. With various groups in the camp I spend the four hours permitted me.

Together we visit the Quaker shop, a little building large enough to accommodate some thirty or forty men at the long benches which run along either side. At these benches are to be found men working at inlaid boxes of various shapes and sizes, at carving picture frames, or perhaps at building or rigging a model ship. In the middle of the room the men have improvised a hand lathe, which, though it requires the combined efforts of two men to work, is constantly in use. An examination of the work is always interesting and often the means of lengthening the list of my acquaintances.

An inspection of the theater and its equipment is also always in order. The theatricals are in the hands of several able men and it is surprising what these men with the most limited, improvised apparatus are able to produce in the way of stage effects. A charge of a few pence is made for all performances and the money thus raised is employed in purchasing the necessary costumes, etc., for the next production. Already I have been of assistance in making such purchases and I seldom visit the camp empty-handed. The filling of requests for individual men as well as making purchases for the benefit of the whole camp forms no small means thru which effective service can be rendered, and a way opened to larger things.

With regard to the work of the Association at Pattishall, there are three difficulties confronting us. The first is to find a leader among the noncommissioned officers whose Christianity is big enough to bridge the gap which exists in the German army between noncommissioned officers and men. The second is to reconcile, if possible, a small group of pietists among the men with a group of officers who seem cordially to welcome and profess willingness to assist in any move on the part of the Association which promises to benefit the camp as a whole. The last difficulty is to provide meeting places for the numerous educational classes which the men are eager to organize, for the Bible study groups and small religious gatherings, as well as some place free from noise where the men may write, study or read.

Of these three difficulties the first perhaps is the most serious as on its solution depends to a large extent the solution of the second. The difficulty of finding rooms for the Association can be met by utilizing the dining hall in each of the four compounds. We have been granted permission to erect two partitions in each of these halls, forming thereby eight good-sized rooms for our use with a class room and a reading room in each compound. The only drawback to this arrangement is that the rooms must be cleared for the use of the entire camp at mealtimes.

A call on the commandant completes my visit to Pattishall, and a walk across-country and a train ride finish the day.

Tuesday there are the accounts to be looked after, errands to be run, and purchases to be made on behalf of the men in the camp, with a German lesson in the evening.

With Wednesday there comes another train ride of nearly five hours, which brings me to the picturesque little town of Dorchester in the south of England. After a hurried lunch I load up with several dozens of oranges, grapes, and cigarettes and present myself for admission at the gate of the camp, which lies on the outskirts of the town. A visit to the commandant, the first thing in order, is one of the pleasures of the visit, for that officer is one whom it is a privilege to know. Courteous, kind, and considerate, and showing a splendid Christian spirit, he does credit not only to his office, but to the nation which he represents.

As I leave the commandant's office I am met at the door by the Y.M.C.A. secretary, a prisoner, who conducts me to the room where he has lived now for so many months. There he calls in his friends and we have a short talk after which we adjourn to the hospital, fruit in hand. There are somewhere near one hundred men here and a visit to them is the main feature of my brief stay within the barbed wire. Their faces always brighten as we enter. To each man we give an orange or some grapes and two or three cigarettes, stopping as we do so to enquire how he is getting on and trying in our poor way to cheer up those who, perhaps, have lain on their backs for months.

Frequently at my expense I have unintentionally provided entertainment for these men; this happened on my last visit but one. The commandant in his friendly way had accompanied me on my visit to the hospital and with just pride had shown me how well the hospital is equipped. During our inspection of one of the wards, we passed the cot of a man suffering from stomach trouble, and nothing would do but that the commandant, who only recently has had his appendix removed and has been a new man as the result of it, must stop and suggest to the man that he undergo a similar operation. As there was no interpreter present and the commandant can speak no German, he turned to me to act in that capacity. The flow of German which resulted was both faulty and ridiculous and the circle of listening convalescents ever did increase, their faces rather unsuccessfully hiding the pleasure which they took in the proceedings. But who could begrudge such men a few moments of amusement even at some slight embarrassment to oneself?

After our visit to the hospital comes a brief inspection of the Y.M.C.A. hut, which contains a large reading and games room, used also for religious meetings and illustrated lectures, two class rooms for the use of the educational department, a quiet devotional room, a store room, and a small committee room. The library is also housed in this building and the whole hut forms a most attractive center.

A parting word with the commandant, and I am off for Blandford, a town some thirty miles distant, where I spend the night, and set out next morning to hoof it to the camp, a good five miles out of the town.

Of my three camps I hold Blandford dearest because in a sense it is more my own. At Dorchester I am carrying on the work which other men began; at Blandford I was the first visitor and knew it when no Association existed there. Thanks to the leadership of a splendid Christian, Feldwebel, we have there now a most active and promising Association. Rather than have us build a hut, the government kindly appropriated a large hall entirely for our use. This we have provided with partitions, dividing it into three good-sized rooms, which we have equipped with cupboards, tables, chairs, etc., and are continuing to make both attractive and comfortable. One of the rooms is occupied by classes all day, fourteen subjects being taught; one is set aside as a quiet room for reading and writing, and the third is used for games, etc. Religious services conducted by the leader are held every Sunday, and during the week there are two large Bible classes. A membership fee of one dollar per month is charged of those who can afford to pay and a certain number of those who cannot are permitted to use the rooms free of charge. This immediately puts the Association there on a basis which will soon be self-supporting. On the occasion of my last visit I found the large rooms filled and the rule of absolute silence during the morning being strictly observed.

[44]

After a couple of hours' conference with the leaders here I have dinner with the commandant and officers, after which I visit the hospital where I distribute fruit and cigarettes. A short time spent in brief visits with different men rapidly consumes the four hours allowed and I find myself about the middle of the afternoon headed for the station. A long ride and a late arrival in London complete the day.

Friday resembles Tuesday even to the German lesson in the evening and on Saturday I catch up on the pile of work left over from the day before. And so it goes, with Sunday as nearly as I can make it a day of worship, of rest, and letter writing.

CHAPTER III

THE spring months of 1917 were for Harold Gray months "in the wilderness." From them he finally emerged after having fought through to certainty in a new understanding of the nature and mind of God, an understanding which brought revolutionary changes in his own life.

The focal point of this experience was the seminar paper which he prepared for the round table of secretaries at their April gathering.

It must not be forgotten that Gray had in earlier letters stated his hatred of war and his belief that the method of force was unchristian. To that declaration, however, thousands would have given ready assent, for many of the men in the trenches and many of the civilians at home sincerely hated war and counted its "necessity" an evil. But at the moment, hated evil though it was, it did appear to be a necessity, the less desirable of two undesirable choices. And as such they gave it their hearty support.

The problem for Gray was that a nation or an individual could espouse an evil, even tho it be the lesser of two evils, as a means to an approved end. He was persuaded that an alternative of good must be available, and he set himself with persistency to find the answer to the question which saints of other days have asked, What would Jesus do in my situation?

[46]

He was determined that the answer should not be one sentimentally conceived. To the best of his ability he would think it thru, seeking for the answer in a logical application of the conclusions arrived at thru a critical study of the life and teachings of Jesus.

It was no emotional stagecoach that brought Gray to the position of conscientious objector. Faulty his logic may seem to many, unconvincing his insistent applications of conclusions reached two thousand years ago to situations of our day, but no one will doubt that he brought to his question a mind hungry to know and to comprehend the truth, however much his heart may have been stirred in the process.

April 15

Three weeks is the longest period I think I have ever allowed to elapse between letters.

The exceedingly high standard which my colleagues have set in their papers at our monthly seminars drove me to my books in a fashion which relegated almost everything else into the background with the exception, of course, of my camp work.

Sunday, April first, saw me thru three books and the week following in spite of some excitement found me still going strong. By Saturday night I had my material pretty well in mind with the intention of transposing it on to paper Easter Sunday and Monday. As I started for bed Saturday night an idea struck me which so captivated me that I resolved to alter my whole paper and take a chance on developing an entirely new line in the two and a half days still remaining. The idea was the outgrowth of considerable reading altho I had never seen it expressed in exactly the form which it now took. Easter Sunday and the day following I worked at high tension and by Tuesday night I had the first draft ready for presentation. There were no startling conversions or anything of that sort but the paper was well received and was followed, as might well be expected in view of the subject, by a very warm discussion.

My idea is thoroly revolutionary and if I drive it to its logical conclusion, as at present I am disposed to do, it will result in some radical reforms in my own life. It has made my New Testament a living document instead of a "scrap of paper" to be abandoned when necessity which "knows no law" demands it. The Gospels, particularly Jesus' teachings and the atonement, have become illuminated; God has been refound, in truth, a very living companion. The things which I have been feeling for the past six months but which I have been unable to express are now gradually settling down into convictions. To be sure I have only begun to work things out. I don't know where Christ may lead me before I have done, but God helping me I must go, cost what it may. If this world is to be saved, it must be by those who are willing to get "back to Christ," by those who believe as he did absolutely in the ultimate victory of love and who refuse to sanction any other means for overcoming evil.

[48]

CHARACTER "BAD"

Wordsworth wrote,

> "We look
> But at the surface of things; we hear
> Of towns in flames, fields ravaged, young and old
> Driven out in troops to want and nakedness;
> Then grasp our swords and rush upon a cure
> That flatters us, because it asks not thought;
> The deeper malady is better hid;
> The world is poisoned at the heart."

President Wilson's speech was the finest expression of a cause, which, if war is ever justifiable, is certainly worth fighting for; the rub comes in that "if" clause.

Well, I mustn't spend more time now over this subject altho for me it represents about all that has happened during the past three weeks. My prayer is that in the excitement you have not all joined the mob. I am sure that the voice of the people is not always the voice of God and I think this is one of the times.

With the exception of summoning us to greater effort and courage the declaration of war has had no noticeable effect on our work. My own visits to the camps have continued with regularity with the exception of Monday last when on account of my paper I skipped a visit. Everywhere the men have almost gone out of their way to be nice. Only once the first week was the issue even raised. I was passing out oranges to the wounded men at Dorchester and was stopping at each cot as is my custom if only to smile when one of the men said, "You are at war with us now, aren't you?" I asked him to try to forget that I was an American and think of me only as a Christian and his reply was that I would thereby become "international." On my last visit this man was the most friendly of all. The men seem eagerly to look forward to my visit and it is great to be able to work for them.

It was with a real thrill that I noted Father's handwriting in your last letter. It is wonderful to feel that he is back of me at a time like this. God has always been good to me but His goodness never was appreciated as it has been since I began to realize what He has given me in Jesus and you and Father. It would be a poor sort of man indeed that didn't feel drawn towards love like that.

Some day when I have thought more and rewritten my paper I shall send it on to you. Enough for now.

The paper on the conscientious objector read before the group of secretaries at Mr. Ewing's home has its chief significance in its effect on Gray's own thinking. He was grasping for a social philosophy of living far larger than a formula for the individual's attitude on war; in his endeavor to arrive at the mind of Christ in the regard of God for human personality he was feeling his way in that groping fashion so typically human toward the heart of the Christian message. Moreover, he was demanding that that principle be so interpreted as to have concrete and daily meaning in all the sectors of his living.

Most seminar papers come as interruptions in more or less busy lives, easily forgotten when the occasion has passed. This one sent its author on a path of public ostra-

cism and social disesteem which led directly to the guardhouse, to Leavenworth prison, and to Alcatraz.

Here in brief is the central theme of the seminar paper,
that God never violates the right of choice which He has
given man as one of the characteristics fitting man for companionship with Him, that this eternal respect for man's
right of choice is testimony of God's love even as respect
for personality must be the core of love. Mindful of this
abiding truth, Jesus rejected the instrument of force as a
means for founding his Kingdom and substituted the instrument of compelling love.

Writing from the imagined point of view of a Creator-
God, Gray argued:

"By the very nature of the case it must follow that free
will is essential. To be sure this may result in the men we
have created exercising it by refusing to be our companion
or even by turning against us. At the same time by possess-
ing the right to choose, they share with us in one of our
greatest powers, and at least one common bond is
established.

"But if this right of free choice, which we have bestowed
on man, is to be effective and produce the result we wish,
we must respect it above all else, and we cannot place in
the way of his choosing obstacles which virtually leave
him but one choice. Such respect for personality inevitably
involves tremendous risks yet it is clear to see that unless
it is sacredly guarded the very end we purpose is defeated.
. . . The first act of love towards any man is complete
respect for his right to choose freely, guarantee that his
choice is not forced by us either thru fear or otherwise."

Interpreting "the positive side of love" that makes "the right way so attractive that men are drawn to it," Gray sought to analyze the temptations of Jesus representing them as parables of means or instruments presented to the Man of Nazareth to achieve his Kingdom. The temptation wherein Jesus spurned Satan's offer of world power gave Gray material which he believed had immediate bearing on the problem of war and the Christian's duty. This interpretation became a central life-principle by which he sought to command his own life.

"Palestine at this time was suffering under the heel of a ruthless foreign invader. On every hand Jesus saw his people ground down under a system of taxation, the wickedness of which has probably never been paralleled in the world's history. Furthermore the conception of the Messiah as a conquering king must have come to his mind at this time. It could not be otherwise—many of his contemporaries expected such a deliverer. The experience he had been thru assured him that he was indeed God's chosen; but he was no heavenly being coming on the clouds of heaven—he was a man, a descendant of David. Naturally and inevitably the temptation came to him to call together an army, to fulfill the national hope by conquering the Romans and establishing by force a kingdom of peace and righteousness, in which men should be compelled to do right. This was the simplest, most natural, most obvious of all ways of attaining his purpose. It was the way in which kingdoms had always been founded. Many were attempting it in his own time. Any other man would have accepted it saying 'the end justifies the means.'

The greatness, the uniqueness of Jesus is nowhere seen more clearly than in the fact that he recognized this as a temptation of the devil. Satan had disguised himself as an angel of light. To recognize him thru that disguise was to conquer him. To use methods of violence which could not but stir up anger, hatred, and cruelty, in order to found the kingdom of love, peace, and righteousness, was to use the tools of the devil for the work of God. It is never right to do wrong. Jesus saw this and answered, 'Thou shalt worship the Lord thy God and him only shalt thou serve.' Here we have the direct reply of Jesus Christ to all the specious arguments for using war to bring peace, using oppression or injustice to bring the gospel. As is the end, so is the method. Like produces like. If the kingdom of righteousness, peace, and joy is to be founded, it cannot be founded by injustice and war, and the infliction of sorrow and misery on the innocent such as inevitably accompanies war. . . .

"To believe that men were incapable of choosing the right and must therefore be prevented by force from choosing the wrong would be to deny the spark of the divine Jesus knew to be within them, the very spark that it was his mission to fan into a flame. Only the method of love could serve his ends and tho he undoubtedly saw that in a world constituted as ours is, such a method involved tremendous risks, suffering, persecution and death yet with an unconquerable mind he chose it and Calvary was the price he paid.

"Thus in the Cross of Christ do we find the crowning expression of the Master's love for men and his refusal to adopt the method of force. He had given to the world the best he had and the world hated him and nailed him on a tree because he had refused to be true to his nation and their hopes and to lead them in what would have been the most just war the mind can picture, a war of liberation against the tyranny of Rome."

The words grow stale on paper; for Gray they were ablaze with fire. They had come as handwriting on the walls not of a banqueting hall but of a bedroom in a rooming house in the heart of London. He had slight interest in them as a subject for a forensic tussle, as words to be battered about for the joy of contest; rather they were words of life which he was called upon to incarnate in the flesh.

April 22

Your letter of April 2nd lies before me having arrived two days ago. In many ways I wish I could be home where I could express some of the things I feel, but perhaps it is just as well I am here where I must fight things out alone and come to know my own mind before facing others.

The past week has witnessed a continuance of one of the greatest struggles I have ever known—a struggle which will determine my attitude not alone towards this war but to the whole of life. It is coming to a choice between allegiance to Jesus or to the State when she goes contrary to what I clearly see to be Jesus' commands exemplified in his life as well as in his teachings. There can be no compromise. It must be either the one or the other. I believe we are all responsible for this war and the man who lays the blame at Germany's door has failed to do some clear thinking. Germany has simply dared to go wrong, to carry to its logical conclusions a philosophy which every one of us is only too prone to follow if necessity demands.

This war is the natural result of selfishness which every one of us is guilty of. Pride fostered by wealth and pride's bedfellow, fear, lie at the root of this war, and the Gray family, H. S. G. in particular, carries a pretty good share of sin in this respect; I am considerably concerned with putting matters right if it is not too late.

I am coming to feel that if this world is to be saved it will only be by men who, in spite of countless difficulties, persecution, and suffering, are willing to risk everything as the Master did even if the price is the cross. Indeed it may be that we can save men only by the way of the cross, not by resisting them, but by loving them in spite of what they are. War is the very contradiction of this.

It is a wonderful thing to be alive these days and even greater to be young; may God give us strength to dare to be great!

May 6

Altho two weeks have slipped by since my last letter, practically nothing of importance has happened. Everything is going well. At Pattishall I now have a wonderful little Bible group which I am conducting myself in German. The men are rallying around me as I never dreamed of, and from the point of view of effective work I have done more in the last two or three weeks than in all the rest of my year put together. We have risen above nationality and found Jesus Christ.

Your letter of April 9th arrived last week and frankly it did not bring great joy. Perhaps this war has warped my judgment, but I refuse to believe that it is Christian no matter what else it may be. Naturally I can have little to say as to what the family's attitude should be. I wish you could all support it as little as possible. It must seem awful to say it but over here the Y.M.C.A. and the Red Cross appear little more than parts of the army, efficiency departments as you might say.

What good may come from this war will come as a side issue and not from the direct aim, and even this good will be enormously outweighed by the evil. Once people thoroly lay hold of the idea that in the last analysis force will do the trick, leastways appear to, believe me, there will be the devil to pay. It is impossible to keep one's eyes and ears open and not hear and see things.

There is only one way to drive out evil and that is with good. This world will never be what God intended it until men are willing to stake everything on love, and see that no means, no matter how alluring, which is inconsistent with love can be justified by the end. For two thousand years men have seen the end which Christ came to establish but in their haste they have completely overlooked an even more important element, the means. Not until we restudy Jesus' life and teachings with a view to both the end and the means shall we know either God or man. When both the end and the means are made consistent with love, we shall begin to see men removing mountains. I cannot describe my state of mind. There has been a terrible upheaval and it has brought me to God as I never knew Him before. He has been talking to me a great deal of late and I have been talking to Him. Even tho the present looks so black, it may mark the dawn of a new epoch for the Kingdom of God on earth if only even a few of us will dare to have faith. I have some great dreams, but I cannot tell of them now. May God bless you every one.

When a man, whether great or small, persists in directing his path of living and thinking in other directions than those approved by public opinion, it is frequently said of him, "He is beside himself."

The weeks which followed the meeting of the secretaries' seminar for the discussion of the position of the conscientious objector found Gray still struggling to find his way. Conviction had laid strong hands upon him, hands that could not be easily thrown off—indeed, hands that he had no desire to throw off. His battle was never one of accepting what he believed to be right: it was one of determining wherein lay that right in the particular situations which faced him for action.

There were talks with friends, conferences with Dr. Orchard, who thru these days was serving as his spiritual adviser; there were, too, long hours of solitude for thought and prayer. The crisis came in the Jacob-like struggles of the night wherein, as he wrote to his mother, he seemed to be "struggling with God in order to get free to save society." In his intense sincerity, in his unswerving determination to see an issue thru, counting not the costs, one can almost hear the young American's voice speaking age-old words, "I will not let thee go except thou bless me."

Some have been inclined to speak of these weeks of Gray's life as a time when the strain of his association with the work of the German prison camps and the facing of the issue of war robbed him of his mental poise; others see in them a time when he walked the roadway to Damascus and heard words which were to alter his entire life.

It was probably a fear of alarming his parents that kept him from writing more fully of these experiences in his letters of the summer—that together with a haunting worry lest disagreeing with him as they did on the rightness of the war, they would not understand.

June 17

Nearly two months have slipped by since my last letter home, without doubt the longest period I have ever allowed to expire between letters. At first I did not write because I expected that each day would bring some letter from home which I could answer; this resulted in a wait of over six weeks. Then a certain inertia set in together with a feeling that perhaps for the time at least a temporary estrangement was almost inevitable as a result of my recent change of mental outlook. The two worlds in which we have come to live are so different that even my closest friends are finding it difficult to realize and grasp what has happened to me.

Until a week or two ago my work in the camps continued without interruption. At Pattishall I had a splendid Bible group of some thirty or forty men whom I was leading in a study of Fosdick's book *The Manhood of the Master*. Owing to a rather unhappy experience, I am no longer able to take articles to the camp, which has turned out well as my time is now free for the truly religious work.

At Blandford I had a group of twenty-two men in the same course; Dorchester was the only camp where I was not personally conducting a group. The difficulties to be faced in all our work are increasing daily; perhaps none of these is greater than the intense depression which prevails as the men realize they must face another winter. In fact, the war is beginning to tell on everybody.

I wrote you that I had been doing some hard and painful thinking. For over two months now that process has gone on until the foundations of pretty much everything except my religion have been undermined. My mind has undergone such an earthquake that even my dreams reflect my thoughts. For example, a couple of weeks ago I came in from a lesson very tired and threw myself down on the bed without undressing. I fell asleep and had another of those nightmares. I remember no imagery except that I was struggling with God in order to get free to save society. My struggle was so real that it woke me up and I found myself writhing on the bed still in my clothes and with the lights on. It was a moment or two before I came to myself and realized where I was and what had happened. In one form or another this thing has been repeated night after night. As yet I have not found a vocabulary to describe what has happened nor have I found anyone who can help me. As nearly as I can describe it, it is the birth of a social self or the realization of social responsibility. Previously my religion has been a more or less personal matter having to do with my own inner life and my direct responsibility to other people. Now I am beginning to realize that there is another side, which is responsible for this war and the countless other sufferings of humanity. I am beginning to apply Christianity to everything with the result that either society or Christianity must sooner or later go smash so far as my own life is concerned. When you begin to apply Christianity to your income and its sources, to your possessions and how they were produced, and countless other things, it is clear that either Christianity was never intended to apply to these things, in which case I propose to abandon it, or the very foundations of society are in for an awful upsetting, and then comes the problem where to begin. Obviously the first place is in our own lives. Before we can lift a finger to save society we have got to make our own lives meet the test, a humanly impossible task in the present social order.

I cannot here set forth the results at which I arrived. I began to do the hardest thinking of my life. Finally when I had things fairly well in hand, I went to Dr. Orchard, my pastor and one of the soundest thinkers in England. He gave me an hour one evening and I went to it with all my soul. Every little while he would smile and comment, "How interesting!" When I was finished, I told him I wanted him to jump all over my plans and punch them full of holes. Imagine my surprise when he turned and said, "My dear boy, there isn't a hole in them. I have only one thing to say; you have got to keep your head and take care of yourself. Remember there are others involved in this besides yourself; you must keep your balance. You have got hold of something tremendously big."

A day or so later I turned in my resignation to Mr. Ewing on the following grounds: First, that I was not doing the work well owing to my mind being so completely on other things that I was moving almost in a trance, and furthermore, that I was no longer able to preach Christianity as my own life was consciously wrong and unhappy. Second, that the war and particularly the work in the camps were so getting on my nerves that I could not sleep nights and was generally becoming run down. Third, that I felt the one great need of the present was for men who would think and that the Association with its incessant drive was not giving its men opportunity to do this. There were other reasons, but I shall not mention them here.

Mr. Ewing accepted my resignation as going into effect in the fall, until which time I should keep in touch with the work by visiting the camps only occasionally. At once I began to put my house in order preparatory to a long vacation during which I can recuperate and change my mind if such is God's will. I am perfectly willing to grant that I have temporarily gone insane, but I also realize that a rest is the only thing which will bring me back.

Gray sought that period of rest with new acquaintances living outside of London, going up to the city for visits with friends and occasional periods of work. Here in the little town of Rickmansworth he found simple, homely occupations which kept him actively engaged, out-of-doors, and yet there was in his days time for thought.

July 14

I wish I were where we could have a good long talk together. There are so many things to be said, things which are not always easy to tell in a letter which must be censored. It has been several weeks since I wrote last. Many things have happened which I cannot take time to describe. After a couple of weeks away I am now back in Rickmansworth. I am glad to be back for it is very quiet here, and quiet seems to be the thing I crave now more than anything else.

The past winter has been a hard one, the hardest of my life. My work has kept me on the go from early till late and it has not been easy work. Prisoners are not easy men to work with; their lives are full of suffering not of a physical sort, for they are well treated here in England, but of a mental kind which it is not easy to alleviate. There is much suffering, too, outside the camps, suffering it is not

easy to blind one's eyes to and so much of it is quite un-
called for.

All winter, as you have doubtless gathered from my letters, I have been growing in the conviction that something
is wrong somewhere. The damage which this war is doing
to life and property is insignificant in comparison with
what it is doing to men's souls. It is damning them by the
thousands.

In April, as you know, I had to give a paper before the
secretaries, and chose as my subject the defense of the
C. O.'s. Previous to this time I had done little reading on
the subject and practically no connected thinking. That
paper started my mind to work and it has been going at
full speed ever since. I couldn't sleep more than a few
hours each night and it wasn't long before my reserves of
energy were almost gone. I wasn't satisfied with anything
I read and that seemed to make matters worse. Finally
with God's help I hit upon something which felt like rock
and for some time I worked over it and watched it grow
in my mind, and then in the excitement of the moment
and in a mad desire to get away I resigned from the
Y.M.C.A. and decided to beat it for South America. I
wanted to get away from the war, away where I could do
some manual labor and at the same time think uninflu-
enced by "wars or rumors of wars."

For a time Mr. Ewing feared he would be unable to
replace me at once and so I agreed to visit the camps every
two weeks throughout the summer or until a new man
could be procured. Last week, however, this man was obtained and his passes almost immediately were procured

from the War Office, mine at the same time being recalled. Now I am free, but as so often happens when we sit down to rest we realize how tired we are. I am almost all in. It is nothing which requires any doctors or anything of that sort, just lots of sleep, fresh air, and food. I wish I were at home and yet for several very sound reasons it is best that I stay here.

In the fall I shall either continue here, going back to the prison work, or return to America. I am feeling more and more that you, Father, and I must spend several months together. What interests me far more now is that you and I should get acquainted so that in a sense I can pick up the torch where you lay it down and profit by your rich life of experience.

August 6

For the first time in a long while your letter of July eleventh made me feel that there was still a very strong and close bond between us even tho my life is so full of experiences in which you can have little share and of ideas poles apart from those at home. After all what difference do ideas make where there is love? Indeed when I realize what a terrible wrench it was for me to come to the position I have even tho I am still young and plastic and with a year's experience behind me of which you have not the slightest conception, it is quite too much to expect that you and Father, who have become more set, who have so much more at stake in the present order, and above all who have nothing in your experience to correspond with

what I have seen and heard, that you should see or sympathize with my point of view. It is deepening daily, this
point of view of mine, only I am keeping very quiet about
it. I am almost tempted to call it "vision" because I feel so
sure it is not the work of my own brain. I feel this because
of late I have felt so closely my relation to God. You must
try not to think me a mystic or a dreamer if I say I think
He has a real work for me to do only it is hard sometimes
to be patient and learn instead of getting busy.

Eventually the Allies will defeat Germany and then I
dread to think what will happen. When hatred has been
cultivated in the human heart, it will vent itself on anyone who provokes it and after this war there will be plenty
of provocation. Life has become dirt cheap and we are
teaching the laboring man and everybody that, granted
your end is sufficiently high, force is justifiable. They are
going to remember and when they come to the war with
capital in which they have a ten times more just cause
than we have against Germany, we may hear a repetition
of that tune and then perhaps the music won't sound quite
so sweet. America is jolly near being the capitalist among
the nations. Personally I cannot isolate her motives from
the fact that she is slowly becoming conscious of this fact.
Wealth always requires an army to protect it and many
Americans know this. And an army—well, that means
autocratic power with economic slavery for the masses.
Germany could not have spread her culture more cleverly.
. But then the world was ripe for it. Sooner or later when
men turn from God they find it necessary to worship

something and I suppose the state is as good as anything. In the days of Rome when men refused to worship the state or the emperor who stood for the state, they were martyred. They were good C. O.'s, those early Christians, and they had a faith worth dying for but not worth killing other people for, a very different thing. Perhaps some of us will have to go that way some day but it won't be the worst thing that could happen to us. I would much rather surrender my soul and conscience to God and die, than to the state and live.

The Conscription Bill calling for the services of all able-bodied men between the ages of twenty-one and thirty was written by Congress with the intention of providing opportunity for the conscientious objector to find a place in noncombatant service, but the error was made of believing that the vast majority of these objectors were members of organizations espousing the cause of pacifism. The bill, passed on May 18, 1917, read in part: "nothing in this Act contained shall be construed to require or compel any person to serve in any of the forces . . . who is found to be a member of any well-organized religious sect or organization at present organized and existing and whose existing creed or principles forbid its members to participate in war in any form and whose religious convictions are against war or participation therein in accordance with the creed or principles of said religious organizations, but no person so exempted shall be exempted from service in any capacity that the President shall declare to be non-combatant."

August 14

I do not think the new conscription bill allows for much freedom of conscience. I am not a member of a religious organization opposed to war and I do not intend to become a member of any unless the Fellowship of Reconciliation counts as such, in which case I have no objections to joining for the purpose of exemption. However, if it really comes to a show-down, I am prepared to go the limit before I join up, which may mean anything from imprisonment to being disinherited. My reason, if it is necessary to give one, is simply that my relationship to God is the biggest thing in my life and participation in war is inconsistent with that relationship.

I am feeling more and more that I want to come home. Probably by the time you receive this letter I shall be much nearer a decision than I am now, but at present the future is very uncertain. I am not keen to return to the prison work partially because of the great strain which it makes upon me and partially because I feel so limited in preaching the gospel which I have come to believe.

If I returned, I should want to meet just as few people as possible. The last thing I want to do is preach pacifism. At the same time, as you would soon realize if we had a chance to talk, it would be impossible for me to talk about conditions here or the war in general without revealing my own convictions.

No doubt you have remarked by now how little I realize

the state of feeling in America and how impracticable all these suggestions are in the face of it. Of course I realize that if I returned and could not get exemption on religious grounds, I would have the joy of a winter in prison, but then I can imagine far worse things. It might be a terrible disgrace to the family, but I think I should rather like to go the limit for conscience' sake, and I am quite sure I could face my friends afterwards.

Mr. and Mrs. Gray were doubtless aware of the slight chance their son would have of securing exemption from the draft on the grounds of his religious belief when, in reply to a request he made for advice by cable, they urged him to remain in England.

August 21

The past week since my last letter has been practically uneventful. I have lived in overalls and scarcely been off the premises except to take a walk. . . .

Germany is the only logical nation. We have in her what our philosophy will do for us when pushed to its logical conclusion and only a few Christians seem to be beginning to realize that the law of logic is as necessary to truth as the law of experience or any other law. This war is going to show to the world that Christianity is the hardest task to which a man can turn his hand and that it demands logic; and most of us fear the result if we are logical. It costs. "Courage is not a thing of weapon but of wounds."

The cross of Christ has become the very center of the universe to me. It represents God's way of dealing with sinners and war represents ours. In the old days sin was terrible because God punished it relentlessly. Since Jesus' day and the Cross, sin is terrible because it hurts the heart of a loving Father, a Father who is willing to suffer rather than by violence sweep away man's opposition. How can a man help loving a God who respects his personality like that? No wonder the early church grew, its members had a real gospel.

Please forgive me if I bore you and Father by carrying on like this but sometimes it seems as if I couldn't help it and be myself. If you will let me come home, I will try and be very, very good. Honest!

August 28

Your letter of August 8th and Father's of August 11th arrived yesterday just as I was leaving Rickmansworth to take up my residence again in London. I am still with the Y.M.C.A. at 45 Bedford Sq., and there is little likelihood of my leaving them for some time, if at all, until after the war. For the present I am acting as building administration secretary for new quarters to which we expect to move shortly. While the position is not permanent, it will give me a little more time to think things over and settle upon a definite work. There will be plenty to keep me busy, and I do not believe the work will be too hard. The American Y.M.C.A. is taking a fine building here and their work is likely to develop a good deal. I refer, of course, only to administrative work. I am in no way connected with any hut or building for handling troops.

The summer has helped me much and my friends feel that I look better and talk more sanely. Altho I realize that I was more or less swept off my feet in June, I still have done nothing of which I am in the least ashamed, or indeed would do differently if I had it to do over again. Things have worked out for the best, I think, all along the line.

The letters written during September and October, with their rapid shifting of plans—France, South America, England, America—reveal the painful uncertainty in Gray's mind. In mental turmoil he was rushing from one idea to another, accepting only to reject. Of his position as a conscientious objector there was no question: that was determined. What was uncertain was the course of action which he should take, especially in view of his growing conviction that the war-work of the Y.M.C.A., in all of its numerous forms, except the work among the war-prisoners, was an arm of the Allied military forces and as such potent in the continuing of the war. Should he return to America and wait to be drafted? Should he return and speak openly of his pacific views? Should he find a place for himself in some industrial mission in South America, waiting there until the government called for his services? The opportunity to do Y.M.C.A. work in France was considered and rejected.

It was the understanding of both Gray and his father that as long as he continued as a secretary of the Y.M.C.A., he would be exempt from call by the American local draft board.

September 8

It is Sunday evening just after nine and I have come into our new offices for a while to write. It has been an interesting day. This morning I heard Dr. Orchard preach one of his great sermons, after which I went up and had a chat with him on things generally but especially with regard to the Russian situation.

The most important thing which happened week before last was A. C. Harte's visit to town. He came while some of the other secretaries were out so I had the honor of being his private secretary for the three days he was here, piloting him around. I might say that Harte is the head of all the prison work and now secretary to Russia. He took me to the American Embassy with him where I met Ambassador Page and the three of us sat together for about twenty minutes while Harte unburdened some state secrets. The next day I was privileged to meet Lord Newton of the Foreign Office together with other bigwigs; when Harte met them in conference, I was smuggled in as Harte's private secretary. It was an interesting experience to say the least. I think if I had planned to go to Russia, Harte's visit would have made me want to change. He wants men to go over and by ministering to the Russian soldiers buck up the army. To me, there is no differ-

[71]

ence between that and becoming a soldier, and I shall not discuss my views on such a course.

It is daily becoming more apparent that there is no such thing as a halfway position with regard to war. As Dr. Orchard said to me this morning, "I am awfully sorry for you young fellows, but if you men are really Christians this war will make you, and if you are not it will break you." To him there is no relation between Christianity and war; they are as far apart as the poles. May God be merciful to the broken men; they are here in millions.

I want to cry every time I see an American paper and read how the church at home is calling this war righteous. Good God, do you know what is going on over here? Do you realize that if the truth were told, this war couldn't last another week? Either the world is mad or God is. If it is the world (and we can only find this out by thinking), then what are we doing to bring it to its senses? If it is God, then perhaps the soldiers are right; "go just as far as you like"; any sin is permissible; they will probably be shot soon anyway; give them what they want.

I may be mad but, by Jove, I'm not the only madman. War breeds madmen. If war is wrong, then there is a whole lot more in our civilization that must go. There is no stopping between Germany's philosophy on the one hand and Christianity on the other. The one controls or attempts to control men's actions by smashing their wills and the process is one ghastly nightmare in which both sides suffer alike; the other controls men's lives by winning their wills, in which both sides grow toward each other and God in the process.

[72]

Do you realize that if there is no other way than war, Christianity is a failure, it is a lie? If that is so, I say let's chuck it at once. Let's not preach something which is not true. But if it is true, has a Christian any business to use any other means than that of love for overcoming evil? Father may say this is no time to discuss theories, but, by Jove, he's wrong, absolutely. War is wrong, even as sin is wrong because it violates men's personalities, smashes them, crushes them, and sin cuts the heart of a loving Father. I think it is about time that some of us who pretend to love God stopped giving Him pain and thought just a little.

September 16

After carrying this letter of September 8th around in my pocket for a week, I am prone to tear it up. Please forgive me for what I have written. I send it only because it expresses my state of mind. Many things have happened lately which I should like to write about but cannot now. The old fever is back again. Either I am mad or God is calling me to a great work. I have tried to argue with myself from every point of view and it is no use. I must go forward more and more. I am feeling that I am in God's hands and He is leading me. Where I shall end, He alone knows, but I am quite sure my task is not here. Please just try and trust God and ask Him to guide me. Sometime in the near future I hope to sail for America and to spend at least a little while at home before I go on. If I am called up, I shall simply go to prison. I know that will be very, very hard for you, but obedience to God's will must not count the cost.

September 20

The two letters from Father which I have received, the last one over two weeks ago, have made me very depressed because I have felt down deep that for the first time in my life, for conscience' sake, I might be unable to do what my father wanted me to do. I shall not say what is against his will because I know that his wish like mine is that I should do God's will.

When I got Father's first letter I did as he requested. I went to Mr. Carter and laid the case before him thus: that I was absolutely convinced that war was unchristian as was likewise most of our social order. I said I believed God had given me a definite life work in connection with my beliefs, but I also realized that I was as yet years away from such a work in point of preparation. As it was a question of marking time till the war was over, I wished to be of service if possible and to comply with parental wishes by offering my services for work in France. Carter saw my case, agreed with me that it was compromise and that I was winking at a system both of us believed to be wrong, but felt nevertheless that I had decided wisely. He offered me the religious work directorship of one of the big base camps and requested me to report in Paris on October tenth. The next day I had a chance, by accident, to chat with him for a few minutes and both of us felt that owing to my beliefs and the danger of becoming involved in controversy if I did the religious work, I had better take an administrative post of some other sort. To explain what I mean: a short time ago a Y.M.C.A. secretary in the Canadian army resigned because, as he said, the men asked so many questions about how war could be Christian that he saw that if he continued and was true to his beliefs and answered the men squarely, he would soon be faced with a revolt in the camp, and he was not prepared for that.

For just one week I stuck it and it was the most unhappy week I have ever spent in my life. I couldn't pray and I simply dreaded to meet people. I felt as if God had said to me, "If you go to France, I guess you and I must part company." One night when we had an air raid and the machines were over London for about two hours between twelve and two, I honestly felt so miserable I didn't care whether I got blown up or not. Then one evening Evan Thomas and Maxwell Chaplin and I got together and talked things all over, and when we realized that we had all experienced the same thing, we saw what was wrong. We knew we had been false to our Master. The next day Thomas and I both wrote Mr. Carter explaining our position and turning in our resignations. Thomas has already sailed for America.

Later I saw Carter and tho he was very sorry to learn of our actions, he felt that under the circumstances we could not do otherwise; that if we were untrue to our consciences, nothing was left to us.

I feel that I must go to South America and that I must go within the next year. What I propose to do is to affiliate myself with some mission, preferably an industrial one, where I can work and teach and study until such time as I feel prepared to work out some great social principles on a small scale in a new social order. I know this sounds ridiculous, humanly impossible, and so it is. But there are some things humanly impossible, like Christianity itself, which are not impossible with God. I honestly believe God has some purpose in leading me as He is. Perhaps He is fitting me for something absolutely different from what I expect, but whether I know or not my great concern at present is obedience.

The problem now is this, shall I return home for a short time or shall I try to go direct from here? Personally I prefer to come home where I can talk with missionary boards, etc., and perhaps make arrangements more easily, to say nothing of seeing you all for a time—at least if I am fortunate enough to remain out of prison. I shall have little to say. These are poor days in which to criticize when men by the thousands are giving their lives for what they believe to be right. I admire them all from the bottom of my heart, but that does not mean that I approve of their way. I cannot longer hold the position I am in at present; it is too much like the middle ground of the coward. In the position I am in it is a struggle to keep my spiritual life alive. The things which I hold to be sacred are being smashed around me every day and I am powerless to lift a little finger against it because of my official position and the illogical way of life I am following.

I have been kept fairly busy for the past few weeks furnishing the new quarters and particularly leading morning devotions for the staff.

I hope to sail for home sometime the latter part of October, or possibly if Maxwell returns in December, I shall come with him.

October 15

Mr. Ewing has been very insistent in his request that I continue here as his associate. I know the prison work, and I am getting a pretty fair line on the American work in England, and as Mr. Ewing is heading up both, a very big job, he feels that he needs a right-hand man who knows the work thoroly and can act for him if occasion should arise. It is a tremendous job in itself, and in addition Mr. Ewing wants me to head up the spiritual work particularly among the staff. It is a question only of whether I am big enough for the job.

October 22

For a week now this letter has lain in my desk. It has been a very busy week. Scarcely a night have I been in bed before twelve, going all the while.

In a sense I am very happy here. I have never been with a finer crowd of men in my life than the secretaries here. Practically all of them are strong C. O.'s, which makes it even more interesting. This is particularly true of the men in the prison work. I have been leading morning devotions a good deal, and it has afforded me a wonderful chance to give the very best I've got and then to realize

[77]

how poor I am spiritually. How wonderfully God works! He makes us good by bringing us face to face with holiness so that we are ashamed and yet desire to be like Him. And then how differently man tries to make people good, by attempting to smash all opposition, by trying the futile task of attempting to drive out Satan. When will the world learn that far from stamping a thing out, persecution and war only spread it?

Last week a party of twenty-five American secretaries arrived. I chatted with some of them and for the first time really realized how war-mad U. S. has become. It has practically settled the matter of my return. I had thought of staying on. I am afraid that is going to be absolutely impossible, since being in this work for a short time I am thoroly convinced that the Y.M.C.A. is essential to the cause of the Allies. It is going to be the most important factor in victory—Victory—the word runs a chill all thru me. I fear that word as I should fear hell. God forbid that there should be any victorious nations in this war. I cannot conceive of any greater calamity befalling any nation than victory.

Yes, I am afraid I have got to come home. If I had been sure of going to prison soon after my return, I think I would not have hesitated as long as I have. I have felt confronted with the question of what should I do provided I was left free. I have come at my position thoughtfully and prayerfully and after much suffering as I have realized what my position might involve for my friends and loved ones, yet I have come to it and may God give me the courage of my convictions. If I come home, it will be the hardest thing I have ever done.

God bless you, Father dear!

On October 23rd, Gray's father cabled: "Important. Receive my letter before leaving England." Mr. and Mrs. Gray were eager that Gray should remain in Y.M.C.A. work, either in England or France, so that he might not be demanded for military service by the government and thus forced to declare his position as a conscientious objector, a position with which they had very little sympathy.

October 28

I await with interest the letter from Father to which he makes reference in his cable. Without in any way knowing what he has written, it is hard for me to conceive of anything which would make me change the course of action I have finally decided upon, namely that of returning home. The young men of my day are facing a tremendous moral issue and I refuse to take advantage of a loophole to avoid that issue. The easy thing would be to remain here where I have lots of friends and where I could enjoy many, many pleasures and work with comparatively little discomfort. The vastly harder thing would be to leave those who agree and sympathize with me, face the sea and return to a war-mad country in order voluntarily to face an issue, which for a time at least I could avoid, and perhaps as a result to face prison or if not prison a far worse fate, the hostility and persecution of my home and friends.

[79]

One thing I am quite sure of and that is that I cannot ally myself with an organization which is making it easier on its own confession for the governments of the Allies to carry on this war. And indeed one does not need the confession; his eyes and ears are enough if he will but use them.

How tired you must all become of my theorizing! It seems so hard these days to write about the common everyday events and yet I know they are the things you are really interested in. I am living at the Central Y.M.C.A. by myself. The little room is just large enough to turn around in, with a cot, a small dresser, and a chair. I don't spend much time in it so it hardly needs to be bigger. I usually get up about eight in the morning, have my cold bath and breakfast, and get over to the headquarters in time for prayers at 9:30. After that it is a question of opening Mr. Ewing's mail and looking after as many matters as I can without troubling him. Then there are errands, etc., which keep me full up most of the day. Whether the job is one which I would care to take as a permanent one, if I had no conscience, I do not know, tho I question it. One thing it has given me some idea of this war work. I am seeing it from the inside and I am more and more disappointed with it.

October 30

The reason I have written so little is not because I do not love you; it has been more because I have felt that my powers to put things in words have been so small and the chance for misunderstanding so great that I have been afraid. Then, too, in the face of the great principles which I have been facing I am dreadfully afraid I have let lots of little things slide. I am beginning to realize this and I am going to try very hard to change. I shall try more to write about the little things, the everyday things of life because they are all of interest to you just as much as some of the other things.

I await Father's letter with interest, to say the least. I do not feel that I can long remain here because I do honestly feel that it is God's will that I return.

The promised letter was slow in coming. It was not an easy letter to write, and Mr. Gray seems to have been loath to bring himself to it. It was finally written on November 28th, a long letter of paternal affection and solicitude expressing, however, almost complete disagreement with the views which Harold had recently espoused. The letter affords a full and clear expression of the state of mind of the Christian gentleman of 1917, the average American at his best, who saw the war as a necessary evil, destined to yield a fruitage of peace and goodwill.

November 28

Dear Harold:

It is no easy matter to write this letter to you, in fact so difficult that I could not send it to you when I intended. To be sure I have been driven hard for time; but it has been a problem in my mind what would be wise and effective to write you. When I sent you that cablegram, October 23rd, we had received that day a letter from you saying that tho you might not come home until December, you were likely to come any time. Mother and I are just about frantic to see you, for you know we love you so, but we know the serious situation of affairs here, and we could not possibly approve of your coming home at this time. So I cabled that day that you might not leave England and I fully intended to write you at once, but it became physically impossible to get that letter off; and then other letters arrived from you and in each case we would come to some new conclusions as to what was best to do, and just how to write you. I regret more than I can tell you the unavoidable delay in sending this letter, and I know you have been daily expecting it. . . .

"After the war" may mean many years or perhaps not a very long time, but for the present let it be understood that you must not come home until after the war. This means a sore privation to you and to us, but it is only what the war is doing to millions of homes in the world today. In our case it is temporary separation—but in what untold cases it means permanent separation! I must express myself frankly—very frankly to you. Mother and I are greatly distressed at the views you have come to hold, and we want to save you if we can from the inevitable suffering and regret which these views will later bring to you. You have been placed very close to some phases of the war, much closer of course than we, but you have not been able evidently to get a broad world vision of the horrible thing; you have not had the proper perspective, as well as being too young, to keep a well-balanced attitude towards it all.

You have been put under terrific strain, we know, and we cannot but appreciate how it has all come about, and we sympathize with you—we do not censure—but you must come to see things differently. You say you are a "Conscientious Objector"—a C. O. There isn't a friend that your mother and I have that isn't also a C. O. Anyone who doesn't object to war can't have my friendship or respect. War is frightful beyond words. "War is hell" just as many times as you want to say it and then some, but worse than war is having in the world the merciless, inhuman, brutal German organization, fattening on bloodshed and destruction, and determined to stifle as fast as it can free peoples and free institutions everywhere. This wild hog of the world must be captured and its power for unspeakable crime and injury taken from it. . . . It cannot be reasoned with, it is beyond reason. It has become a power, a law unto itself without any regard whatever for the rights and privileges of any other people. It is utterly outside the pale of civilization and is today the most completely outcast nation the world has ever seen. To be sure, it is a wonderful nation because of the blind confidence the people seem to have in their infamous government, and because of its resourcefulness, intelligence, and organized power, thus standing a strain which probably no other nation in the world could have stood. But this does not lessen its guilt or in any way excuse it. It stands today the greatest criminal nation ever known, and its frightful record impossible to erase. . . .

You say you hear America is war-mad. This is absolutely not so, America was never saner than just now. The speed with which she is getting ready to leap into the breach to help save the world from the monster in this present awful struggle is a marvel to all. There is no division of opinion here. President Wilson and the government are backed up by the people to the last degree. The people here are not crazy; they are calm, serious, determined, expecting awful days are coming and that they must be met with fortitude and heroism. America knows she has an awful and a lamentable piece of business to do, the necessity of helping to clean up with this ruffian of the world and she'll not wince. You may be sure the job will be well and thoroly done as far as America is concerned. No one of any influence or consequence, not even the hundreds of thousands of drafted young men in training camps question that America has taken the right course, the only course open to her in this world crisis and under all the circumstances. Germany has gotten beyond any other language than the language of shot and shell, and it is impossible now for the world to do other than speak to her in this same desperately terrible language. Nothing short of that can possibly make her understand or put her where her filthy hands can do no more harm to the world.

What would pacifism do now? What could it do? Pacifists in America now are looked upon as shy mentally—"nobody home"—because they can't see or be made to see the true situation and what a calamity it would be to stop the war before the goal is reached. This is not unchristian; it is the only attitude left for an intelligent, farseeing Christian no matter how much he regrets the taking of such an attitude. Pacifists in America are linked up in the public mind with anarchists, socialists, labor disturbers, pro-German agitators, the whole bunch being a menace, an aid to Germany and a drag on our government in the hour of sore trial. The public mind regards no difference between them all in their hindering, blocking effects, and tho pacifists are not generally interned or put in jail, all the others are being interned and jailed as quickly as possible and so a great multitude are already where they can do no further harm. Pacifists have to keep their mouths shut, and where they don't do so, they are soon brought up with a round turn, are fined, or told by the authorities "where to get off." Pacifism in this great crisis is disloyalty to the country, and the country is fast spotting all these pacifists, hinderers, and other disturbers, spotting them thru the tremendously increased detective forces and thru other means. The utter lack of patriotism of these objectors can't long be hidden and their usefulness and the esteem for any of them are practically at an end now and for years to come. Pacifism in theory and generally in practice is fine and should not be exterminated. Pacifism certainly has its use and place but its place just now in this tragic hour is asleep on the shelf. Pacifism would have the war stopped now. God be praised if it only could be, but now and before the goal is reached means another greater war twenty years or so from now or as soon as Germany could get her plans and equipment ready and raise to military age the millions of baby boys—war-babies—legitimate and illegitimate born in the last two or three years or yet to be born, thus suggesting shameless, unprincipled conditions and practices which no other nation now fighting her

[85]

could or would match. In this connection her treatment of women in war-occupied territory thru unspeakable lust and debauchery and for cruel, merciless war-ends will shame her thru hell forever.

Righteousness and truth must prevail, and if they can't be established on the earth without fighting for them, they are worth the fight. If what far too little righteousness and truth there are on the earth now are likely to perish from the earth or at least be greatly diminished, then if no other means can save them they are worth fighting for. "Peace at any price" in the face of such a desperately wicked power as Germany means that she will dominate the world and America be in the hell-pot with the rest of the world, under her iron heel. Surely you are not so much of a pacifist as to want that. America would never have existed, would not have had the proud history she has, and would not be the justly conspicuous nation she is if George Washington and his followers had been pacifists. Nothing but fight freed the colonies back in 1776, absolutely nothing else at that time could have lifted England's injustice to those thirteen colonial states. I grant you there were pacifists then but they were only in the way, were of no use in that vital struggle and most of them had to clear out. I understand a great many of them sneaked to Canada to get away from the trouble and it is only recently that a Canadian friend of mine told me of the many descendants of these pacifist-refugees of the Revolutionary war-time who live in Canada and are jealous of this country's greatness and influence.

Is there any greater name in the history of the world, not alone America, than Abraham Lincoln? He was a conscientious objector to war and shunned it with tears but he was up against a condition that could not be righted without that awful period of America's history, the Civil War. "Peace at any price" then would have meant the northern and southern states as two nations today, slavery in full swing all through the south and doubtless a great deal in the north, and the justly glorious name of Lincoln would be unhonored and almost unknown. And there were pacifists in the north at that time too, but how discredited they became, a target for suspicion and ridicule. Those people got themselves out of joint with the country in a crisis and never could get back in line again. Their pacifism or their southern states sympathies were continually thrown up at them as long as they lived. After the Civil War the men who were in it either as fighting men or helping civilians became at once the men of affairs in the country and that is exactly what is going to occur after this war. Pacifists and all such who have hindered rather than helped will be shunted on to a siding for keeps, where they can continue to watch the main line of influence and achievement occupied by the men who have been active somewhere in the present great struggle—the struggle which is sure to mean so much to the immediate future and all the future of the world.

If you were at home and going out for a stroll some day chanced to come up to your sisters being brutally handled by a ruffian, what would you do? What should a pacifist do? Indulge in a little verbal argument? Such as, "Do you know it's very wrong for you to do that?" "You should do unto others as you would have them do to you," "I shall get very angry if you don't stop," or "I'll call the police right away," or a lot of other good remarks in their place but utter nonsense under such a condition? Why, my boy, while you were handing out the dirty brute such a line of talk, he'd have the laugh on you and hand you your knockout. As Germany understands only the language of shot and shell and cannot be reached by the gospel of love, so such a low-down street brute is far beyond the influence of the gospel of love, and understanding only the language of slugging must be treated at once accordingly. There is nothing to do but wade into that kind of a cur. It's unpleasant of course; no room for argument on that point, but it would have to be done to save your sisters. If you didn't defend them in such a crisis, you would be discredited and scorned all the rest of your life. But defending them you would establish yourself as courageous and manly and would entitle yourself to a hero's acclaim. You have but to shift the scene to the larger stage—the world—and look upon Germany as the unprincipled thug who should be waded into at once without ceremony. It is an awful thing to kill a man, yet in the case of the low-down villain I have pictured, merely to wound him or knock him out temporarily means that like all other criminals under similar conditions, he'll lay for you and come back at you some day. So Germany, the great criminal nation, if she is merely temporarily hurt or knocked out, will lay for the world and come back strong some time. Germany as she is should cease to exist, but the world would stand for Germany as a democracy, as a republic, just as soon as she could be sure she wasn't loaded, for Germany is the most intelligent, tricky nation ever known.

You are not to blame for the war, and neither are we, but in some way the accumulated sins of the world seem to be reaping their awful punishment in this war form. True Christians, though not responsible for the war, have a call for service in it just the same. Godless peoples, some wearing the cloak of Christianity, are surely in large part responsible for the war but their doom is fast approaching. I don't see how America could do anything else but enter the war, but suppose for the sake of the argument that she has made a mistake, we must stand by her, and you must be game, be a true American and stand by her too. In a recent letter you stated that the sight of the American flag used to thrill you but now it doesn't. I am grieved to have you express yourself in such a disloyal way. What's the matter with you? Are you turning into a socialist, with no use or regard for flags or governments? If you are headed that way, you are headed for the breakers and oblivion. Christ distinctly taught loyalty to one's government. An American Christian should love the American flag, for it is the most beautiful emblem in the world and stands for more than any other. Don't ever come back to America lagging like that in your love for your country and her flag. Brace up and get a different vision if you ever want to come home to be loved and useful.

This war offers the greatest opportunity for real service which I suppose has ever existed and I surely want you to serve somewhere, not duck it all, and thus nullify the splendid year's work you did put in. I want you to continue steadfast in some form of "Y" service for which you are so well fitted. Not German prisoner service for I fear that has done you harm and accounts in part for your present losing and groping your way.

Of course, this war is not God's will. It is the work of the Devil, and yet I believe that out of it God's will will be done in the earth as never before, and His glory will come to fill the earth as we have never known it. Just how I can't tell you, but the war is surely linked up with prophecy and a new world will emerge from it, the old order of things largely having passed away. This is surely a great eternal wave of history making. Don't try to run away from it but get into it for service, and be made by it. Your attempt to buck it, to stem the tide will simply be pathetic and hurt you. To bail out the ocean with a pail might illustrate the influence you can have. A mosquito can hurt an elephant about as much as you can make headway against the present world situation.

As much as we want to see you it would be unwise for you to come home now. You would almost immediately have to report for service somewhere and get into uniform. Thousands of just as good young men as you are thus offering themselves to their country. Thank God that there are so many who will do it! How they will be honored later on! But you say you will not fight, that you will go to prison, or face the firing squad before you will join the colors. Oh, please come out of it, and don't continue in that line of thinking and believing that will lead you to pull off some such silly martyr-stuff as that. You would soon go to a training camp after coming home and refusing to fight you would be put at unpleasant menial service such as "chambermaid" or kitchen scullion or some other equally elevating duty for a boy of your unusual talents. This line of menial service in the training camps they say becomes so offensive to the C. O.'s that they are generally very quickly willing to join the ranks and be spared the contempt and ridicule of the regularly enlisted men.

I want you to link up with Carter on his staff for France, or anywhere else he thinks you can best serve. If you come home, that will put you definitely out of the "Y" service and will oblige you to join either the army or navy. If you come home with pacifist views—well, you'll simply have to keep your mouth shut. But if you come home with such views, then I will feel obliged to go to France or elsewhere myself in "Y" service. Where you object to the thought of the "Y" being vital to the cause of the Allies, I rejoice in it. I am strongly tempted to go over anyway next spring or along about May or June first, when I can get my affairs into shape to leave.

I believe in prayer, and I fear I do not pray enough, but I believe it is possible for a man to pray too much, or to pray with preconceived ideas of what he wants to do or intends to do and subsequently believe that God has answered his prayer in accordance with his wishes. He has not given God a free hand to work in him and guide him but he has gone to God with the program all set. I wonder if anything akin to that has occurred in your case. Isn't it barely possible? Go back to God and ask for His further guidance and see if He may not show you that your duty just now is not to escape some form of war service but to do such service. Our Bible school lesson next Sunday is "Nehemiah Rebuilds the Wall of Jerusalem"—Nehemiah 4:1-23. I wonder just how pacifists reconcile verses 13-18.

I have no doubt it is as you say that in war time untold evils spring up where comparatively few existed before, and tho war brings a value in its enforced discipline and economy along many lines and tho it brings out a wealth of deeds of valor, heroism, sacrifice, and service, yet if it is to be judged by what it is when it is on the stage, then nothing justifies it, for these values I mention can be obtained thru some other means than thru bloodshed and mutilation and sorrow on sorrow. But it is from the results it brings as the years pass by, that war must be judged and justified. We are constantly meeting and talking with American citizens who have returned from a visit to poor war-worn France and also returned wounded soldiers, so we are not without getting some very reliable first-hand information. . . .

Now Harold, don't throw me overboard in your esteem and love because I have written you so frankly. When you come home, be it sooner or later, I want you to come home with honor and much achievement to your credit, not to be discredited and cast into the discard. Hence have I written you thus.

My love to you,
Your father, Philip H. Gray

A month had elapsed between the cablegram bidding the young "Y" secretary wait in England and the writing of the promised letter. Mr. Gray had delayed that he might marshal at leisure the arguments which he believed would move his son from his attitude of stubborn insistence. But by the time he was ready to send his letter, composed with such evident care, Harold Gray had acted upon his own initiative.

The letter, alternately pleading and demanding that he remain out of America for the duration of the war, must have passed him somewhere in mid-ocean, as aboard the *S. S. Orduna* he was sailing for home and uncertain destiny.

The decision to return to America had come late one night in London as Gray and Evan Thomas had sat in Gray's room plagued with their vacillation, yet lacking assurance in which direction courage pointed and duty lay. Neither of them was under any known external compulsion to return although each, should he return, would probably be drafted during the winter. Gray reached for a little book, familiar to them both. It was a book by Mrs. Henry Hobhouse, *I Appeal unto Caesar,* setting forth the situation of the English conscientious objector with case

[93]

studies of men who had suffered prison sentences for their convictions. Both Thomas and Gray had read it many times, had indeed, memorized certain of its passages. From its pages, Gray read aloud the case of Clifford Allen.

A Bristol and Cambridge man, Allen had given himself to the Labor Movement, helping to found the *Daily Citizen*. The Appeal Tribunal had refused him exemption on the grounds of conscientious objection and when he had ignored the summons to service, he had been arrested and sentenced after courts-martial to two years of hard labor. Gray was reading excerpts from Allen's defense before his third court-martial:

"I have before previous courts-martial stated my belief that the method of warfare is socially and morally wrong, whatever the pretext for which it may be adopted. But in addition to this belief I wish to make it clear that I cannot take any share in military work in this war, because I believe there is no substantial reason to prevent peace negotiations being entered upon at once. . . . If I hold that war and militarism are evils which will only cease when men have the courage to stand apart from them, I should be false to my own belief if I avoided the dangers of military service only to accept some safe civil work as a condition of exemption from such service.

"This country is faced with the most insidious danger that can confront a free people in the claim of the State to dispose of a man's life against his will, and what is worse, against his moral convictions, and of his service without his consent. A war which you can win only by the compulsion of unwilling men and the persecution of those who are genuine will ultimately achieve the ruin of the very ideals for which you are fighting.

"You can shut me up in prison over and over again, but you cannot imprison my free spirit. The duty of every citizen is to serve his fellow-men. In all humility I believe I am being faithful to this obligation of citizenship by pursuing my present policy."

Slowly, thoughtfully, Gray reread the last paragraph. Then turning to Thomas he said very simply, "For me, at least, Evan, it must be America."

November 24

I am on board the *Orduna* and hope within a few hours to be bound for America. I have not written or wired of my coming because I wanted to spare you the worry and anxiety of knowing that I was at sea. I am not in the least afraid myself and I have never felt so happy in any decision. I feel sure that I am doing God's will because His presence seems so close!

I am leaving for America because I feel that in this great hour of need pure unselfish service is not enough. What men are crying for is salvation, the salvation which alone comes thru Jesus and his way of the Cross. If I were to preach or live this way to men as I shall sooner or later be impelled to do, it would hurt the Association here a great deal, I mean in so far as they are connected with the army. Therefore, since as a Y.M.C.A. secretary I cannot proclaim the salvation of the Cross without apparently misrepresenting the principles of the Association in the eyes of the people, the only honorable course is for me to resign. If anything happens to me in crossing, you must have faith and believe as I do that it is all for the best in the divine plan.

CHAPTER IV

GRAY'S departure from England, when once the decision to return home was made, was hastened by
the need at that moment on the part of the Y.M.C.A. for
a man to accompany a wounded soldier. The soldier, a
free-lance American who had joined a London regiment,
had seen action in France and had on several occasions
been wounded. His last injury, however, had left him
partially paralyzed in his left side and wholly paralyzed
below his waist so that he was practically helpless. A year's
stay in a London hospital had brought no decided improvement, and there had followed the official decision to
allow him to return to his family in America. Upon hearing of the case Gray agreed to act as nurse and companion
to the man on the return voyage.

The episode is deserving of mention in such a narrative
as this for the additional insight which the acquaintance
afforded Gray into the undisguised brutality of the war
and the falsity of propaganda. The young soldier, a sergeant in his regiment, had had as his special duty the leading of a squad of men after each charge of the company
for the purpose of braining the enemy's wounded. For this
purpose they were equipped with clubs set with steel cogs.
This practice was a safety-measure, employed by both the
Allies and the Germans, to prevent an attack from the

rear, when the soldiers had advanced, by those feigning death.

It may have been in response to Gray's shudder that his companion added, "Of course you get spattered with blood and brain, but you soon get used to it."

With these words burning in his mind Gray returned to hear from his American friends of the "inhuman Hun" who had stooped so low as to brain the wounded of the Allies in unspeakably savage fashion, making use of a heavy club set with steel cogs. The charge was undoubtedly true—but it was a half-told story.

It was war-propaganda of this nature, propaganda to which England had been by no means a stranger, that met Gray upon his return and confirmed him in his certainty that controversies could never be settled with justice thru the means of war-violence. He was forced to listen to stories, widely circulated, of the unspeakable conditions of life in the prison camps of Germany, stories which pictured existence for American prisoners as far worse than death itself. And yet Gray had had in confidence from the lips of an English ecclesiastic who had worked in the chief prison camps of Europe and had returned to England, just prior to Gray's sailing, after an evangelistic tour of the prison camps of Germany, the statement that if he had to choose between living in the prison camps of England or in those of Germany, he would quickly choose the camps of Germany. And Gray had first-hand acquaintance with the camps of England.

The months of waiting between the time of landing and the call from the draft board did not find Gray in argu-

TUESDAY

24

JULY 1973

JUNE 1973						
S	M	T	W	T	F	S
					1	2
3	4	5	6	7	8	9
10	11	12	13	14	15	16
17	18	19	20	21	22	23
24	25	26	27	28	29	30

AUG. 1973						
S	M	T	W	T	F	S
			1	2	3	4
5	6	7	8	9	10	11
12	13	14	15	16	17	18
19	20	21	22	23	24	25
26	27	28	29	30	31	

– APPOINTMENTS –

8:00

8:30

9:00

9:30

0:00

0:30

1:00

1:30

2:00

1:00

1:30

2:00

2:30

3:00

3:30

4:00

4:30

5:00

6:30

MONDAY

1973	JULY				1973	
S	M	T	W	T	F	S
1	2	3	4	5	6	7
8	9	10	11	12	13	14
15	16	17	18	19	20	21
22	23	24	25	26	27	28
29	30	31				

23

JULY 1973

mentative mood. He steadily resisted any temptation to expound his position in public, choosing to wait for the day when he could exemplify his convictions in action.

On June 5, 1917, Harold Gray's father had met the government's demand for the registration of all men between the ages of twenty-one and thirty by registering for his son. This registration caused some misunderstanding since the papers did not show that the registrant was out of the country and on August 5, 1917, orders for a physical examination were issued. On October 30, 1917, the registration was canceled "on the ground that he [H. S. G.] was registered by his father while he himself was out of the country."

On December 12, 1917, soon after reaching Detroit, Harold Gray personally registered, making claim for exemption on the ground of conscientious objection. Fourteen days later he mailed his questionnaire, to which was affixed this statement:

"After sixteen months in England in work as a Y.M.C.A. secretary among troops and prisoners of war, I have come to the conviction that war is absolutely contrary to the life and teaching of Jesus Christ. Out of loyalty to him I feel that I must decline all forms of service in any system or organization whose avowed purpose is the taking of life and the violating of the sacredness of human personality.

"Furthermore I feel that as God works in human society thru the individual conscience of its various members, we are in danger of hampering His will unless the majesty of conscience is at all times scrupulously protected. When the state claims the power to compel men against their wills, and what is far worse against their moral convictions, to support institutions and commit acts which they believe to be wrong, it is not only on the road toward blocking the action of God's will in human society, but it is in grave danger of achieving the ruin of the very ideals for which the nation stands."

Having been classified as A-1, Gray was in turn summoned for his physical examination and, as a result of this examination, made January 28, 1918, he was reported as physically qualified for general military service. After three months of waiting he was ordered to entrain on April 26th and on the evening of that day was received at Camp Custer.

This is a skeleton of dates for the months between Gray's return to the United States and his reception at Camp Custer, with the omission of an incident which reveals his steadfast purpose. He had been previously ordered to report for service on March 29th, but Mr. Gray of his own initiative and through his own influence had secured a postponement of this order for one month. It was his intention to find for his son a desk job in Washington, far from harm's way and the necessity of obnoxious labels, and to that end he had bent his efforts with success. Great and almost bitter was his disappointment when Harold pointedly refused to accept desk work in Washington, insisting that if he were to deny his conscience he would far prefer military service to a cowardly safety-job; great and almost bitter, too, was Harold's chagrin when he learned how completely his father had misinterpreted his motive and the life-principle, so great in his own eyes, for which he was making his determined stand.

In a letter to a friend (undated) Harold Gray speaks of the pain of misunderstanding which both he and his parents were suffering.

My return home was naturally a blow to the folks altho they were glad enough to see me after nearly a year and a half of separation. But both realized that whereas in England I could easily have avoided conscription and the consequent participation in the war,[1] now I would be forced to join the army or do some form of war service. Neither of them fully realized what I had been thru or the depth of the conviction to which I had come, and naturally the thought of having a red-blooded son who refused to serve his country in her hour of need and preferred to go to prison instead was a pretty hard blow.

That first week at home was rather difficult because our experiences and ideas seemed such poles apart. I often found myself getting excited, which did not improve things. But in spite of much lack of tact, I have gradually brought them at least to see that there are two sides to the question and that they cannot ask me to surrender my conscience, for when that goes there is nothing left.

I did not realize until my return how tired I was and

[1] Gray was in error here, for in September General Crowder had issued orders that activity in the Y.M.C.A. should not exempt men from military service.

accordingly I have more or less been forced to take things rather easy. Last week, however, I did slip down east for a week, in order to attend a large Student Volunteer convention at Northfield. I had a fine time and came home greatly inspired and encouraged.

From now on, until we move to our new home, I shall probably remain at home. After that I expect to go to New York to take up some special courses of study and to work in the student department of the International Y.M.C.A.

Instead, however, the weeks of the winter of 1917-1918 were spent in recuperating from the experiences of the months in England and in a study of typing and shorthand at the Detroit Y.M.C.A.

Beneath these activities ran the persistent questions which had to be faced: Where should he make his stand for what he believed to be right? Should he refuse to register? Early he had answered this at his father's insistence by complying with the law. Should he refuse to report for his physical examination? Apparently this was in his mind for a time for there is in existence the draft of a letter (apparently never sent) addressed to the local draft board, insisting that for religious reasons he cannot comply with their order to appear for examination. Again at the expressed wish of his father, he agreed to be examined. Should he refuse to report at the training camp? Others of like faith had chosen this course and had been dealt with by civil law. Again it was at the persuasion of his father that he decided to report at Camp Custer and to accept at the camp such treatment as the government saw fit to mete out to the C.O.

> Custer Barracks
> Battle Creek, Mich.
> *April 27, 1918*

It is shortly after three. I have just had a delicious sausage sandwich and have begun my career as a C.O. As soon as we arrived and had had roll call, I reported myself as a religious objector. I was immediately taken to special barracks where I found one other C.O. out of our crowd, a follower of Pastor Russell. The men with whom we have thus far had dealings have been exceptionally courteous. I was prepared for quite the reverse. I have not yet had my interview with the captain who has us in charge but so far as I can learn from others here I shall probably be allowed to have my books. Of course they will all be examined, but since most of them were written before the war and have no bearing on it except as they bear on life in general, I have no fear but that they will get by all right. There certainly are some interesting looking cases here with their long hair. I sure am keeping funny company. I don't know much about what they believe but they seem to be willing to pay the price of trying to live up to it, and that is the thing that counts.

New men have been coming in all day so there has been little doing in the way of discipline. I have not yet been examined as to my views. I was vaccinated and had my first typhoid inoculation, which has left my arm rather sore. I have read a good deal and talked some with the

men. Most of them take their Bible with painful literalness. There seems to be no one here who goes at the
problem from a modern point of view.

Unless I am willing to accept noncombatant service, it
looks like Fort Leavenworth. I shall be given some command and refusing to obey, I shall be court-martialed.

We are having perfectly wonderful eats and lots of them.

Mothers' Day
May 12

Two weeks have gone by so fast it is hard to realize that
I am a week behind in my correspondence and yet there
is a good deal to write about and it seems as if I had been
here a much longer time. To begin with, I am very happy
and this not only because I feel that I am where God
wants me under the circumstances, but also because I am
being treated so much better than I ever expected to be.

The Monday morning after I arrived I was called down
to the office where I had a long talk with our captain, who
is in charge of the C.O.'s here. As soon as he learned that
I was a Harvard man and had been abroad, his attitude
towards me changed noticeably and the interview became
a most friendly affair. He was interested in my experiences
abroad and asked a lot of questions about the situation in
England. Then he asked me some of the stock questions,
what would I do if a brute attacked? etc., etc., for all of
which I had my answers. I guess he saw pretty quickly
that I knew my ground for he never followed up his
questions with a discussion. He said there were about
twenty "absolutists" in our company who had refused to

accept noncombatant service of any kind, but that all of them were doing their share of the work in connection with the care of the barracks, the cooking, etc., but only that which had to do with their own upkeep and welfare. I could see no reason for refusing to share in this work, at least until I had given it a trial and had come to the conclusion that it was not the wisest policy, so I consented to do my share of the work here in the barracks, but under no circumstances outside the barracks. This means that I take my turn in the kitchen, washing kettles and pans, go on fire guard, and one or two other things. So far I have only been on duty once and that was in the kitchen washing kettles all day. I have helped sweep and straighten up the barracks nearly every day but this was not regular duty.

I do not anticipate much trouble with the captain; he told me he had a great deal more respect for an individualist than for some member of a religious body into which a man might be born and whose stand he had simply accepted as a matter of course with perhaps the full support or even under the pressure of family and friends. I think he saw that my case was very different from the average. What the government will eventually decide to do with us, it is hard to say, but for the present as the captain expressed it, "they are trying to kill us with kindness." From the point of view of the government it is by far the wisest policy. They have won over by means of such a policy many who would otherwise have stood out absolutely against all service. A man has got to know his ground pretty well to be able to resist kindness. I am being fed here almost as well as at home. I guess there are thousands in the American army today who never have been fed so swell in their lives. For example today we had thick tomato soup with rice, the kind I like, white bread, real butter, boiled potatoes with lots of gravy, roast pork and dressing, stewed tomatoes, and the most delicious strawberry shortcake you ever ate. With the possible exception of the shortcake, we had more than we could eat of everything. Of course today is Sunday, but it is almost as good as this every day and every meal. They sure do know how to cook in the army!

Perhaps the hardest part about the life here is the lack of privacy. I am living with about seventy others in a room not much over fifty by thirty-five or forty feet. The bunks are iron with straw mattresses, placed in four long rows running the length of the room, the bunks being placed side by side about a foot apart. The blankets are warm and the sleeping is good. We get up at about six o'clock in the morning and all line up in front of the barracks for roll call. At 6:30 we have breakfast and then clean and straighten up the barracks for the day. Usually those who are not on duty (I am referring to the C.O.'s) are set to some task of absolutely no military value, which would not be done unless we did it, like washing the windows every day or some such job. The purpose is to keep us active and from moping about, altho personally I think there would be little danger of the latter taking place. In spite of this work we have a good deal of spare time, both in the morning and in the afternoon. After supper we usually play indoor baseball in the court at the side of the barracks. We have heaps of fun and it is good exercise. All of us are confined to barracks and are not allowed more than a few feet away from them. The only walking we get is round and round the barracks.

There is a great bunch of men here, I mean C.O.'s. None of them wear uniforms or accept pay. They represent some odd faiths all right, but they have got their hearts in the right place. As I think I wrote before, the trouble with most of them is that they take their Bibles with painful literalness and to hear them talk you would think the story of Adam was of equal importance with the crucifixion. However, they are not all like that, and whether or not they have much use for my beliefs, I certainly have no difficulty getting a hearing with any of them, especially when I get to talking about war. I have been disappointed not to find any Quakers or I.W.W.'s here, the former, because they come nearest to representing my own faith, the latter because I should like to convert some of them.

I guess there is no questioning the fact that the C.O.'s are the happiest men in camp and their happiness is not make-believe. It has been a long time since I have done so much laughing or had so much fun as I have worked. Nearly every evening the boys get together and sing hymns. We could not ask to be in a better place so far as making converts is concerned. We may not talk much with the other men in the company, but we are being watched and it is clear to see there is a spirit at work. From the point of view of the Kingdom I think it is far better we be kept here than that we be released. If we were released,

[107]

a lot of slackers would undoubtedly join our ranks. As it is I think there is little chance, and we can do much to make converts. There may be little to show for it now, but we are sowing seeds which are going to bear a harvest some day.

It is Mothers' Day and of all the men who have reason to be thankful for the mothers they have I think I have most reason. Certainly she never meant so much to me as she has these last few months. My stand has been very hard for you and you have been simply wonderful about it all, and believe me, I love you for it and for what you are, one of God's noblewomen. I am afraid I am one who talks a lot about love and then does little to show it, but then I always was the chief of sinners and that in spite of all you have done for me and been to me. You must forgive me and keep on trying to make me better.

May 18

To look out of the window you would think Camp Custer was located in the middle of a desert. The air is fairly white with dust. Everything in the barracks is coated and all but the C.O.'s who are confined to barracks, have left for the woods or fields. It is going to be pretty bad here in the summer time. The combination of heat and dust is going to make life mighty uncomfortable.

Yesterday I had my first sick day in years. In the morning I was inoculated for typhoid for the third time since I arrived, and it sure did get me. My stomach was in bad shape anyway, I guess, and the injection tipped it off. I have got to be more careful about my eating. I am eating too fast, too much, and getting too little exercise. It takes just about eight minutes from the time the men sit down to table to the time they get up. They don't dine, they just feed.

The more I see of army life the deeper grows my conviction to oppose the whole business. What a mess men are making of life and what a huge amount of precious energy is going to waste in this awful business! The time is not far distant when they are going to be pretty hard on the C.O.'s here. Already they are beginning to tighten up. A day or so ago when I was putting in twelve hours scouring pans in the kitchen for the second time this week, the other C.O.'s, who were not on duty, were ordered to carry some supplies for the Quartermaster's Department, and when they refused we were deprived of our privilege of playing ball.

I have just stopped writing for the last half hour to listen to one of the craziest arguments I ever listened to between some of the C.O.'s and some of the soldiers; the C.O.'s sure did make themselves look like fools. I took no part in the argument myself, I was almost ashamed to. Surely most of these C.O.'s have half-baked brains and it is hard to be classed among them. On the other hand a few of them are great spirits. I have made some friends here that I shall not soon forget.

Last Tuesday or Wednesday a man arrived here after ten months in the Detroit House of Correction for not registering. It is almost impossible to believe that such conditions as he described could be true in a land like ours. He is a Quaker and an I.W.W., just the kind of man I have hoped to meet for a long time. Of course, we do not agree when it comes to the methods which his organization is using. He is accepting noncombatant service but will probably be stationed in our barracks where we can talk together off and on. He is a University of Michigan man and perhaps the brainiest fellow here, but he has let his brains lead him into agnosticism. It is curious how so many of the socialists are agnostics, principally for three reasons. (1) They see how the church has been used by capitalism to its own advantage and twisted all of Jesus' teachings to fit its own purpose. (2) They have been thru so much suffering that they cannot reconcile evil in the world with a just and loving God. (3) Science and evolution have completely undermined their faith in the Bible and no larger faith in God has ever come to take its place. When people have talked about the inspiration of the Bible, they have thought of verbal inspiration and not inspiration in its broader sense.

Your big envelope of letters arrived last Thursday. Believe me, it was great to hear from home and friends. . . . I never know when I may leave here, either for the guardhouse or Fort Leavenworth. In many ways I would rather go to the latter place than stay here. Some of the men have friends there in the Disciplinary Barracks and they have a far more regular life than we do here. . . .

I have been practically all afternoon writing this letter simply because I have been interrupted by argument and discussions on every hand. It is well-nigh impossible to think connectedly for more than a few minutes at most.

Sunday, May 19

The world looks fairer today. We have just had supper. This morning one of my best friends, a Mennonite, who was stationed in the kitchen for today, had his family put in an appearance; he asked me to take his place, which I did gladly. I wish you could see the dinner we served. It beat any Thanksgiving dinner I ever ate. I can remember only some of the things, but there was thick rice soup, roast chicken, mashed potatoes, creamed carrots, creamed peas, gravy, bread and butter, onions, delicious fruit salad, three kinds of pie, ice cream, coffee, etc. Everything was cooked to the queen's taste and we actually turned in at the end of the meal serving dishes untouched, including even the ice cream. I guess the reason was, everything else was so good that by the time the ice cream got around they sat "chuck full of soup."

This afternoon I played truant and went out for a good walk; we were gone about two hours; we visited a lake and had a boat ride. They have never said anything to me about being confined to barracks altho they have spoken to all but two of the other C.O.'s, and these latter have been willing to do odd jobs outside the barracks. It was with them that I went for my walk. I am going to go out from now on until they speak to me. The worst they can do is to send me to the guardhouse or Fort Leavenworth. Meanwhile if I don't raise the question, they may let me alone. If they don't stop me, my lot will be a great deal better off, both from the point of view of exercise and change. I can get off by myself too and read. I have absolutely no fear of either the guardhouse or Fort Leavenworth. I wish I could feel that you folks at home felt as little anxiety about my future as I do. I feel myself so completely in God's hands that worry and fear are unknown to me.

June 9

Can you all come out to camp sometime this week? I am to be shipped to Fort Leavenworth the first of next week and that probably means that we shan't have another opportunity to see each other in the near future at least. It looks now like a court-martial and a term at the Disciplinary Barracks. I am enclosing Secretary Baker's proclamation regarding the C.O.'s. It is pretty plain. I am glad they have decided what to do with us.

The Saturday after you were here we went for a dandy fourteen-mile hike around the camp. Sunday I was on duty again in the kitchen for the third successive Sunday. I wore my overalls and after serving a huge dinner, I was stopped by the captain who laughingly wanted to know "where I got that suit of underwear." It led to a fifteen-minute talk on things in general. He was very apologetic about not having had more time to spend with you and Father.

Tuesday morning I was called into his office to be cross-examined by a captain from headquarters who had just had a wire from Washington requesting that a statement of my position be sent on at once, I have no idea what for. After talking a little while the captain suggested that I draw up a statement of my position, which I proceeded to do. I was not in a writing mood, but towards the end of the day I turned in as brief and comprehensive a statement as I could. The next morning the captain called me down and asked me to enlarge certain parts. Then I showed him my long statement. Immediately on reading it he asked me to incorporate parts of it in my statement to Washington. The result was rather a patchwork and not at all as I should have written it had I had more time. The captain made several suggestions about arranging the parts and making corrections. He seemed anxious to have me make as good an impression as possible.

Wednesday evening I was put in charge of the C.O.'s and took them out for a hike. It was the first time we had been away alone without a noncommissioned officer and we had great sport. Thursday I was on kitchen police all day and Friday and Saturday I had free. Saturday morning I was detailed to sweep out the captain's office. The walls were very dirty and in suggesting to the captain that I clean them, I found myself permanently detailed to keep his office clean.

Saturday afternoon I was again put in charge of a C.O. hike. Before we left, the captain called me into his office and on promise of secrecy I was told that orders had come thru from Washington to have us all sent to Fort Leavenworth in ten days. The captain wanted me to know so I could have you pay me a parting visit. The news as to the exact day of our departure is not known outside and you must not mention the fact to anyone.

Mr. and Mrs. Gray visited Camp Custer during the week-end following the writing of this letter.

June 25

Well, here I am still with no information as to when we are to leave. If you have been holding up any mail for me until I might get to Fort Leavenworth, you had better send it on. If I have left when it reaches here, it will be forwarded.

The past week has been one of the most fruitful since I have been here. In spite of the fact that I expected to leave almost any time, I got twelve long letters off to friends. It is by all odds my highest record for anything of that sort. It would be strange if this prison game should make a letter writer out of me, wouldn't it? I have always looked upon my failure to keep in touch with friends as my besetting sin and wished I could conquer it. Perhaps with God's help I am going to.

The past week has also been fruitful in a deepening friendship with some of the soldiers. When I first came most of them treated me coolly, but that attitude is now beginning to change to one of friendliness and even confidence. I never realized how closely some of them were watching my life until lately when some of them have opened up. Believe me, the greatest sermon a man can preach these days against the war is just a life! No Department of Justice can silence that.

I am very, very happy. It seems sometimes as if God was almost too good to me. What a glorious thing life is, isn't it? It seems as if every day that went by made me appreciate it more. God seems very, very near to me.

There is little news to write. I have had a bad cold all week, but am beginning to throw it off now. We have taken some great walks. The country hereabouts is beautiful and it is a great relief to get out into it away from the dusty old barracks. It has been very dry lately and nearly every day has seen a dust storm. On two or three occasions everything in the barracks has been buried under a fine white powder.

Last Tuesday, I think it was, we were all rushed into fatigue uniforms, otherwise known as overalls, and together with several other companies doubled out to an old railroad siding. The urgency with which everything was done led us all to believe it must be some pressing emergency, and when the C.O.'s were asked whether they would be willing to work for a day we all consented. Almost immediately afterwards I began to feel uncomfortable about it. When they finally marched us to a coal heap by the side of a track and asked us to shovel it back, I began to feel still more uncomfortable about it. When noon came I spoke to some of the other C.O.'s, and we all decided to report back to the captain. Altho the sergeant who had us in charge had no authority to let us go, I took the law into my own hands and together nine of us marched back to barracks. We were a sight, covered from head to foot with coal dust. Immediately on arriving back at the barracks I reported to the captain, who had heard of our coming and was waiting for us in the hall. "I have returned with eight other C.O.'s, sir. We don't feel that this is an emergency situation at which we can consistently work one day and refuse to work every day." He smiled, I think more because of my appearance than anything else and said, "All right." You may lead C.O.'s to labor but you can't make them work!

It seems that the cause of the trouble lay in a mutiny in a Negro labor battalion in which they beat up a lieutenant and nearly killed a sergeant. As a result they were being confined to barracks and we were sent out to do their work. The other men of our company have been at such work every day since. The feeling among the Negroes is very bitter. They are up at five every morning and driven like slaves all day in labor gangs. They can't see this wargame for dust.

There are a great many more men in this old army who are not at all comfortable about the whole business than I at first realized. The life is best fitted to keep men from thinking very deeply but in spite of this fact discomforting thoughts will arise in men's minds. How thankful I am that I had a chance to think the thing out before ever the storm broke or I should be where millions of others are today. The thing seems to boil itself down with most of the men to one of two things, lack of any clear thought about the meaning of life and about the problem of sin and suffering, and the fear, when they do see that war makes things only worse, of not being thought brave or wise or good. Christ is the only solution for both these difficulties because he alone gives meaning to life and he alone can supply the power that will break the bands of fear. When we lose ourselves in him, the fear of what people may think loses its hold. We are no longer slaves but free, and what a glorious freedom it is!

The conscientious objectors of the World War were for the most part willing and eager to accept the alternative of noncombatant service. Their conscience forbade them to participate in war, but they did not find themselves untrue to their best understanding in engaging in such endeavors as the ambulance corps, the farm service, or the relief and reconstruction work under the Society of Friends.

There was a small group, however, of the conscientious objectors who received the name of "absolutists" for the reason that they refused all form of alternative service whatsoever. Many of them came from the smaller, conservative religious sects, the Mennonites, Dunkards, Russellites, etc.; others took this position on moral and religious grounds. Their argument was that altho these noncombatant services relieved them of participating directly in the task of killing men and indeed dissociated them from the military organization of war, they were arms of that service and immensely potent in furthering its success. The absolutist was determined so far as was humanly possible to divorce himself from any activity which in any way contributed to the maintenance of the war.

With this small group of absolutists Gray aligned himself.

His weeks at Camp Custer saw him trying to find words to express the theological and philosophical foundations of his position. The examining boards were asking for statements and he wished to have one ready, phrased with thoughtful care, that full justice might be done to his stand. Moreover, many of the friends who had admired his position against war were doubtful of his wisdom in refusing such forms of humanitarian service as were offered to the noncombatant conscript, and it was in his mind to give a reason for the faith that was his, for their sakes.

The long statement which he had in mind to prepare was never finished. It was to have been a studied treatise on the ways of God as exhibited in His justice and His love, shown in the atonement, and the necessity of unconditional surrender to the will of Christ, as it was revealed to the individual.

Those portions of the statement that were prepared repeat the thesis which he had presented in his seminar paper before the group of secretaries: man was made for the companionship of God, a companionship which becomes farcical unless to man is given the right to refuse that advance. God never forces that companionship on man against man's will, ever allowing him freedom of choice. War in that it attempts to bend or to break a man's will instead of endeavoring to win his allegiance by the attractiveness of the right is a method basically contrary to God's way and God's will.

He arrayed his arguments against war: "the first casualty

in war is truth"; war revives animal passions and instincts, incompatible with personality at its best; war attacks the sacredness of personality at its most vital point, the will, seeking to "break" the will of the enemy; war brings suffering in its degrading effects without the protective or redemptive forces inherent in suffering.

The official boards before which Gray appeared must have listened with amazement and incomprehension to his statements. They were men confronted with a concrete, difficult situation; he was an individual attempting to grasp a theory. They were men struggling with the problems of 1918; he was a man seeking an understanding of a timeless principle. They were men who thought they were dealing with facts; he was a solitary figure who thought he was handling that which includes all facts and is greater than facts, Truth. They and he represented two poles of the world's thought.

July 1

The special board appointed by President Wilson to dispose of C.O.'s has been here today. They dealt with the C.O.'s in short order. I think practically all were deemed sincere on the captain's recommendation, and as all but myself were willing to accept farm service, there was little difficulty.

It was Judge Stone, I think, who conducted the interview with me. Evidently my case had been discussed previously for he seemed to know all the facts. He was exceptionally nice, said he took a special interest in me because I was a Harvard man, so I take it he is the same. There were no questions regarding my attitude toward war. The whole discussion, if it could be called such, centered around my refusal to serve the government in any capacity whatsoever. I frankly admitted that the problem of the individual's relation to society and how far a government was justified in conscripting in time of peace was one on which I had much to think out. But I felt that at present the highest service I could render my nation was in protesting against a course which she had taken and which I felt certain if persisted in would mean her ruin. All admitted that by refusing to serve in any way and going to prison for it was the strongest possible way I could protest. I have been sentenced to Fort Leavenworth, there to be retried with the others including Evan Thomas whom Judge Stone mentioned by name.

Father dear, I know this hurts you; that is the hardest part about it all. Still you would rather have me be true to myself, true to the highest light that I can see even if I am wrong, than to have me do that which at present I feel to be wrong, wouldn't you? And I do honestly feel that for me to take any other course than that which I have taken would be going back on the "still small voice" within. Since you were here I have tried to rethink this whole problem of alternative service. I have prayed a great deal that God would guide me, that if a veil shut out the truth, His Will, He would lift that veil. But the more I have thought, the deeper has grown the conviction that His Will for the present at least lies in martyrdom rather than service.

When I returned from Europe, it was with a very deep

conviction that God had a great work for me to do and that I must waste no time in continuing my education in preparation for this work. I have not talked much about it at home. Perhaps it was a desire to keep my air castles to myself until I could build foundations under them. Perhaps I may never see these dreams realized. It may be that God has only given me a glimpse of a distant future to show me the necessary steps towards it and to give me the courage to take the first step. And that first step is to work for the breakdown of a conscription which prevents men from doing what they feel to be God's Will. No man can serve two masters and if in a man's endeavor to render supreme allegiance to Jesus Christ and to do his Will, family or friends or country become a barrier, I believe he must sacrifice them, and if need be, oppose them. When the state prevents a man from doing the Will of God and he turns around and does the will of the state, is he not deifying the state if not in words then in action by making its will supreme in his life?

If God never conscripts men against their wills to serve Him and His Kingdom but always seeks to enlist them, has the state the right to do what God in His greater wisdom does not see fit to do?

Father dear, it is hard sometimes to think that we cannot see things just alike especially in regard to those things which seem so vital to both of us; still you are of the older generation and I am of the younger and it may be that that divine discontent which is born in each succeeding generation makes it inevitable.

I wonder if it may not have been just this thing which

Christ alluded to when he said, "I came not to send peace on earth but a sword," for you notice the division which he speaks of is always between the older generation and the new, between father and son, mother and daughter, not between brothers and sisters.

If we are part of a great evolutionary process which will go thru all eternity, for a new generation to be at peace with the world, satisfied with it and not striving for something better, would inevitably spell stagnation and death.

Father, in spite of our difference, perhaps almost because of it, I think we have been drawn closer together than ever before. The whole family is coming to mean more and more to me every day. God only knows how I love you all. It may be a long, long time before any of us can know for sure whether I have done the right thing. It is a long-distance race I am running. Even extremists sometimes help the world by calling attention to its faults thru exaggeration.

Inasmuch as the orders for the C.O.'s to be transferred to Fort Leavenworth were not forthcoming, permission was given Gray to spend the Fourth of July with his parents in Detroit.

July 14

Having written everybody else today I guess it is about time I wrote the most important person of all. It is wonderful to have such friends as I have and it is great to hear from them, but it sure does take time to write them.

CHARACTER "BAD"

After leaving you at the end of a glorious Fourth I was fortunate enough to land a seat in a crowded coach and during the course of the three hours and more which followed I succeeded in snatching a few short naps. Shortly after three we were unceremoniously dumped down in Battle Creek with not the sign of a bus or auto running. I ran into a sergeant I knew and together we waited for about three-quarters of an hour for a bus which never came. At last we succeeded in boarding a crowded trolley which dumped us near camp about half past four. A nap which lasted until 5:45 A.M. completed the night.

Under ordinary circumstances I would have been able to sleep most of Friday. Things started out all right for fairly early I and another C.O. were sent to fill a couple of bed sacks with straw. The process usually involves emptying a dirty bed sack first and the dumping ground is a short way from the camp. On this occasion when we had emptied our ticks, we stretched out our clean ones under a tree and went to sleep. When we returned to barracks about ten o'clock, inspection was over, and we took to our bunks for another doze. At noon, just after dinner, we were ordered to pack up all our belongings and be ready to move into a new barracks.

When my own possessions were in order, I was detailed to help clean out the new barracks. It had been previously occupied by a colored company that had just left for some port of embarkation for Italy. You never saw such a dirty place. I worked in the kitchen and in the evening was put in charge of a gang which worked till nearly eleven. Saturday morning we had to stand an inspection by the major.

I have been reading some Russian short stories by masters like Tolstoi, Gogol, and others. They seem to have a soul, revealing a depth of insight into human nature which is sadly lacking in most American literature. Do you suppose you could pick up and send me a stray copy of Tolstoi's *Resurrection* and *My Religion*?

July 18

An hour ago I was ordered to pack up for Leavenworth to leave at once. It is pretty short notice. Father's letter of July 17th was just handed to me. You had better hold up all mail that comes until I can write you from Fort Leavenworth. The instructions from Washington read that I am to be returned to Camp Custer after the trial, but I think this is based on the supposition that I will accept some sort of service.

CHAPTER V

ON JULY 18, 1918, the long-expected orders arrived for the absolutists, all of whom were refusing to accept noncombatant service, to proceed from Camp Custer to Fort Leavenworth. At Leavenworth the group was called before the examining board and the several cases heard. The stay at Leavenworth was brief, and on July 25th Gray, together with a company of C.O.'s, was sent to Fort Riley, a training camp in Kansas.

Gray's first letter from Fort Riley received harsh treatment from the censor's brush; it was, however, the only one of his letters known to have been deleted during this entire period. Concerned by the rumors of the strictness of the censorship at Fort Riley and eager to have his parents informed of his activities and his reason for them, he wrote a long letter on August 7th describing fully the events of the preceding weeks and mailed it at a civilian post office. This letter with its narrative of action and background of crowded thought adequately replaces the briefer letters written earlier.

The weeks at Fort Riley were a period when decisions were becoming increasingly difficult. At Camp Custer Gray had declared himself an absolutist; now for a time he was persuaded he must go still further and refuse to aid the government in any way in maintaining himself. It was a position to which he came slowly and with some misgiv-

ings. The constant pressure of the army officials to force the
C.O.'s into situations which would compromise their stand
militated against calm, reasoned thinking. Moreover, the
new situations which were daily arising called frequently
for immediate decisions. At Camp Custer there had been
the incident of the day when the C.O.'s had marched out
willingly to assist in an emergency only to find that the
need was less demanding than they had been led to expect,
whereupon some of them had returned, protesting, to
camp.

Altho their position of objection was declared and accepted, the men were finding themselves in a welter of
intellectual and practical difficulties. Should they obey any
command given by an officer? Was obedience a condoning
of the system they were determined to resist? If they were
willing to maintain order and cleanliness about their cantonment, who should decide the boundaries of their
grounds? What if the officers were to declare that the entire camp was within their province, whereby they would
be doing police duty for themselves and their brother-
soldiers as well? If they were to assist in the preparation
of their own food, what was to prevent those in charge of
the kitchen using their services for the preparation of food
for the other barracks? And if this took place, as it had
done in previous situations, what was their answer to the
retort, that if they could cook for the soldiers they could
do ambulance or farm service? If they were forced to cook
their own meals, just what was their status in the army?

The decision to which Gray and his closest friends came
was arrived at most certainly more under the pressure of

hostility from officers eager to trap them into a compromising situation than from unimpassioned reasoning. "Those of us who mean business have got to draw the line somewhere," Gray wrote to his father. "To the man outside no matter where we draw it, it must seem petty and arbitrary, and it is ever so much less worry to draw it at no work whatsoever for the military even when we ourselves are to benefit."

It was their utter sincerity and their devotion to their cause that drove them to this extreme position; it is, however, doubtful if they were fully aware of the dangerous individualism toward which they were tending.

August 7

If this letter reaches you, it will be because I have succeeded in mailing it in Junction City, Kansas, without its first going thru the censor.

I hardly know where to begin because I am ignorant of what you may know; therefore, perhaps it would be best if I went back to the very beginning of things even at the risk of repeating.

My departure from Camp Custer on July 18th was very sudden. The whole 23rd company was expecting to move into new quarters the next day, and I had been sent over in the afternoon to get the captain's office cleaned and ready when that gentleman sent for me and informed me that I had about half to three-quarters of an hour in which to dress and pack up for Leavenworth. It meant some hustling. Practically all my friends were over at the new building and did not know of my orders. Only a few drifted in just as I was leaving, so I had almost no opportunity to say good-by to anybody. The last minute I tried to scribble a line to Mother, but I did not have time to finish it.

My guard, a sergeant, was a rather uninteresting sort, a foreigner who had been running a slaughter house in Lansing before he was drafted. He, like myself, had had almost no time to get ready and had been given no instructions as to the character of his charge. We left Battle Creek for Chicago late in the afternoon and at my expense had a nice dinner on the diner. From Chicago we took a sleeper for Kansas. When we boarded the sleeper, we discovered a secret service man in the car; seeing him rather worried my guard. He had been rather afraid of this and for that reason had insisted on sleeping in the same berth with me, but when he discovered this gentleman who might report him if he did not fulfill his duty strictly, he was in doubt as to whether he ought to go to bed at all. We finally arranged it to his satisfaction by turning in handcuffed. It was a rather uncomfortable night for both of us. We had to change trains fairly early the next morning and from then on it was a day coach. We reached Fort Leavenworth about eight P.M.

Fort Leavenworth is quite a good-sized town. The camp and Disciplinary Barracks are about a mile or so from the city. The barracks to which I was assigned was full of C.O.'s from all over and I immediately began to inquire for my friends. Evan Thomas was there to greet me, and it sure was wonderful to see him again. We almost fell on each other's necks. The barracks were three stories high, large and spacious with great balconies running around each story. Evan and I sat up till after midnight talking.

The next morning, Saturday, I went before the examining board and gave them my final answer, a flat refusal to consider any form of service whatsoever under conscription. The examination was very short as they had been over my case before.

On Thursday, July 25th, the whole crowd of C.O.'s at Fort Leavenworth, some one hundred twenty in number, was shipped here to Fort Riley. We were quartered in a large stone barracks, barely large enough to accommodate the entire number comfortably. Several of us were bunked on a fine broad balcony overlooking a fertile valley with sort of hills beyond. It was a delightful place to sleep. Friday we learned that our quarters were not permanent and that we would be expected to build a cantonment for ourselves, clear a field, erect tents, tear down, move, and reërect two barracks to serve us as mess hall and kitchen, build a latrine, install a drainage and plumbing system, etc., etc., and all this to be done under the direction of a couple of civilian workmen. Well, over half of the men, including myself, refused to do this work.

There were two main reasons for refusing. In the first place, I am being held by the government and prevented from doing what I feel to be God's will, and under such circumstances I do not feel that I can conscientiously coöperate with the government in keeping me here. Three courses are at present open to the government: either they must let me go free and thereby admit that the government has not the right to conscript men against their conscience or to prevent them from doing what they feel to be their highest duty; or they must imprison me and publish to the world the fact that religious and political freedom is only a myth in the United States; or they must take absolute care of me for the duration of the war and by that I mean provide me with cooked food, clothing, shelter, and the means of keeping myself clean and healthy, and in the providing of these things I refuse to coöperate with them. In civil life as a free man I should feel it my duty to coöperate, but not here when I am dealing with the power which is defeating what I feel to be God's purpose for my life.

The second reason for refusing to build the cantonment was that we had not the slightest assurance that we should live in it for long after it was finished, or that soldiers and the army might not then have the use of it. Those of us who mean business have got to draw the line somewhere. To the man outside no matter where we draw it, it must seem petty and arbitrary, and it is ever so much less worry to draw it at no work whatsoever for the military even when we ourselves are to benefit.

Saturday morning a meeting of the C.O.'s was called at which Evan presided. It was over the matter of K.P. [kitchen police]; this service an ever increasing number of men was refusing to do on the grounds that they were serving a number of noncommissioned officers and a number of noncombatant C.O.'s. Furthermore many of the men felt that the government ought to provide men to help in the kitchen just as it provided cooks. At Camp Custer I expressed my willingness to do my share of the work until my case had been reviewed, in other words, during a temporary situation. At Leavenworth I served once in the kitchen, but here I began to feel with the rest that if we were going to be dumped off here for the duration of the war, the government might as well know at once what to expect. If you had been at that meeting, you would be able to appreciate what the government is up against. All sorts of conditions were laid down by various men upon which their doing of K.P. depended. It was clear in a few moments that absolutely any agreement or any sort of coöperation among ourselves was impossible. Evan resigned and the meeting broke up.

Saturday evening after supper fifty-six men, including myself, who refused to do K.P., were separated from the rest, were ordered to pack our bags and march out to a vacant lot adjoining the camp. Here we were dumped down with unerected tents, absolutely no toilet facilities, with a single hydrant about a block away for all of us to wash at, and with no kitchen. We were told that at mealtimes we could go a quarter to a half mile to the stone barracks, draw raw, uncooked barrack-rations, unfit for field service, and draw these rations individually, not collectively, return to the hydrant for our water and wood to build a fire, and then go a couple of blocks further to build the fire and cook our food individually. The idea was absurd.

Sunday morning after sleeping out, Evan Thomas and a close friend of Evan's, Howard Moore, and I set out for Junction City four miles from camp without any breakfast. We got there about noon very hungry. At first I was for having a good meal, but when we got down to business and talked it over, we decided that it was the government's business to keep us and that we would not eat until they gave us prepared food, even if it was only bread and water. Accordingly we had only some ice cream which we felt we would have had in any case. Evan got a letter off to his brother Norman to avoid the censor, and we started to walk back to camp. On the way we took a swim, which rather whetted our appetites. Sunday night and Monday I learned what it was to feel real hungry. Monday night and Tuesday were not so bad altho I began to feel pretty weak.

Tuesday night the officers saw that something had to be done. A meeting was called, and they consented to give us a field kitchen and provide the rations in bulk at the kitchen, if we would cook it. About half the men who had gradually come to see what Thomas, Moore, and I were fighting for refused to cook their food claiming that the government should provide, but the other half consented to cook for us, and we were left without a leg to stand on for we were getting prepared food and were not coöperating in its preparation. If C.O.'s wished to act as government cooks and prepare our food for us, we could not object.

Tuesday evening after seventy-four hours without food I had one of the greatest meals I ever ate, consisting of canned corn, canned tomatoes, boiled potatoes, bread and tea. But the scheme of feeding has on the whole worked poorly. The meals have been very irregular with breakfast from 9 to 10 A.M., wheat cakes, bread, coffee; dinner 3:30, beef stew, bread, water; supper 8:00, cole slaw, bread, tea, no sugar. Since Saturday we have had a slight improvement, but still with much to be desired. The food is cooked in a field kitchen out under the burning sun where there is absolutely no protection against the swarm of flies which inhabit these parts. At mealtimes we line up and receive our rations in our mess kits.

On Monday the 5th Thomas, Moore, and I felt that we could not carry on longer without making protest, so we dressed up and prepared to interview the colonel. However, before we went up, Evan and several other men were sent for by the colonel to interview a major who had been specially sent from Washington to investigate our condition. How he happened to come is not clear, altho it was quite likely in answer to a telegram sent to Washington by some of the socialists setting forth our condition. The major assured Evan that this was only a temporary situation and above all that we were not prisoners altho we have been under guard all the time and unable to leave the lot. This limitation has since been removed, and we are now pretty much free to come and go as we please. Evan came away from the interview feeling strongly that the government did not want to raise the conscription issue if it could possibly avoid it and also that the government would eventually give in to men who preferred to starve and be taken to the hospital rather than be treated like pigs. I guess the major saw clearly that a few of us were dead in earnest and meant business. This is not a negative but a positive position which we hold. We are out to break conscription; this is the very first move in preventing future wars.

What I have written I have intended in no sense as a complaint. I have made my bed and I intend to lie in it. I have tried to give you the facts mainly because they lead up to what I want to say about my stand. To you my behavior of the last couple of weeks must almost inevitably seem very petty and small. Perhaps it is, but I feel that it is the logical and inevitable result of the stand I took months ago when I decided not to back this war and to oppose conscription.

As I see it the situation is something like this: The history of man is a record of his struggle for a larger life, his struggle from darkness into light, from falsehood to truth, in short his struggle for the perfection of life in God. In this struggle truth comes to him from within thru the heart to which God is able to speak when man will listen. He sees a light and struggles to attain it; another sees his effort and he too comes to see the light and to struggle towards it; and slowly, very slowly sometimes, the world goes forward and up, and it does so because in the beginning one man or a few were true to the light they saw and by living it finally enabled all to see.

Probably no man ever saw this so clearly as Jesus Christ whose whole life and teaching were a protest against making the will of the majority the final criterion when it came in conflict with the still small voice of truth within. Always a man must follow the light as he sees it, not as the majority see it, even when such a course leads to one's own crucifixion by the majority. Now what conscription does is to claim that not the inner light but the will of the majority shall govern a man's actions and that the state has a right to demand a man's services and to control his actions—always, of course, giving the man as much choice as to his service as possible. This right I deny. I believe the individual is supreme above the state and that the latter exists for the good of the individual, not the reverse; and I shall oppose the state trespassing on the rights of the individual, not because I feel that the individual owes nothing to society and his fellow men but because he owes the best he has to give, and to give this best is impossible unless he follows the light within for then only can society go forward.

Feeling as I do towards the state or the society which deliberately seeks to suppress the light in the individual, you can hardly expect me to coöperate with any such state or society in carrying out its will of suppression, and this I feel I am doing when I build for them my own prison and by working to keep myself, remove from them the care and responsibility of keeping me. I am here against my will and I do not intend to help the government keep me here against my will.

In refusing the farm service or any alternative service I refused all work for the government under conscription, even in prison. I am fighting for an idea, not to avoid participation in war which I could avoid by taking alternative service. I want to bring people face to face with the real meaning of conscription. I want them to see it as it is, the great obstacle to God's action in human society. I sincerely believe that I can do more to bring this about by refusing to condone the evil against which I am fighting than in any other way. If it costs me my health or even my life, I shall count it a privilege to give them. Millions are giving theirs for what I feel to be a less worthy idea and the world rightly honors such men.

August 22

It is so long since I have written you that I hardly know where to begin. A batch of letters came in from you over two weeks ago and I intended to answer and acknowledge them immediately, but with the heat and considerable absence from camp my good resolutions went to naught. As for forwarding a box of grub, I think you will be able to understand presently why such a gift from home would not be acceptable at the present time.

The news of ——'s collapse was funny indeed. It is a poor bit of testimony to his method of approaching the Bible. I hope he is happy in his change of heart. In a sense I feel greatly relieved. I wrote him a very guarded letter in which I urged him to go as far towards meeting the government as possible and in no way even setting forth my position or urging him to imitate my example. It is possible my letter may have helped to pave the way for his change; if so I am grateful. I do not care to see men join our ranks who are not prepared to see their stand thru to the limit.

The weather here has been dreadfully hot without a bit of rain since we came until last night. Several weeks ago a couple of us discovered a dandy swimming hole, and nearly every day until last Sunday a party of us has beat it off with our lunch and spent the day there. Sunday, the last day we went, I raced one of the best swimmers in camp over a mile and beat him rather badly.

Monday Evan Thomas and I went for a long hike. We walked steadily for five hours at a pretty good clip so that we must have covered sixteen or eighteen miles anyway.

When we returned to camp, we found about sixteen or twenty men refusing to eat until the government would provide them with prepared food. The cooks had gone on strike, as I wrote you I thought they would. The situation here has been both unsettled and unsatisfactory for several weeks past. On Tuesday, after refusing to eat uncooked rations, four of us got together and talked things over with the result that a letter was sent to Secretary Baker, a copy of which is enclosed. The decision there set forth must inevitably come to you as somewhat of a shock. For the sake of you and Father I wish it was not necessary, but the time has come when in spite of every consideration to the contrary, I cannot longer remain passive in the face of a great wrong.

August 21, 1918

HON. NEWTON D. BAKER
   Secretary of War
    Washington, D. C.
Dear Sir:

We, the undersigned, have refused to obey the Selective Service Act under which we have been conscripted into the United States army. Realizing the difficulties facing the government in the question of conscientious objectors, we have heretofore endeavored to comply, so far as we were able, with the provisions made by the President for conscientious objectors.

After having met the Board of Inquiry appointed to decide as to our sincerity and over a month having elapsed, we have now decided, as we are unalterably opposed to the principle of conscription and believe it to be un-American as well as the very backbone of militarism and war, hereafter to resist any restrictions on our liberty under the Selective Service Act.

We are ready and eager to work for society as private citizens, nor do we desire to engage in propaganda work against the state, but only to live useful, constructive lives in society.

We have read the President's order of July 30, 1918, regarding conscientious objectors, and we understand that the government is not prepared to exempt conscientious objectors from compulsory service. We have therefore determined to refuse to eat as long as we are kept from following the pursuits we feel called upon to follow in life. We fully realize the gravity of this stand, but we are determined to starve rather than passively submit to an Act which we believe to be opposed to the principles which we hold dearest in life.

Respectfully yours,
EVAN THOMAS
HAROLD S. GRAY
HOWARD W. MOORE
ERLING H. LUNDE

A second letter written on August 22nd contains this further comment on the refusal of the group to eat.

August 22

The question has repeatedly come to our minds, why should we not carry our fight onto the offensive and refuse to eat at all, preferring forced feeding or death rather than passively acquiescing in being deprived of our liberty and denied the right to live our lives in the light of the truth as we see it. More and more we have come to feel that death is far preferable to a life of slavery in which we would be unable to perform the work we felt called upon by God to do.

But a further consideration has influenced us in our decision, namely the effect which our actions might have outside. Much criticism has been heaped upon Germany during the present war because of her enslavement of the Belgians, and yet if the U. S. government prefers to let some of us who cannot agree with her aims and methods die rather than set us free, wherein will the action of the U. S. differ from that of Germany? If I were a Belgian unwillingly conscripted by Germany and believed that the methods of violence were wrong, I believe that I could most effectively fight her by quietly refusing to do her will and by offering her the alternative of liberating me or letting me starve. Should she prefer to let me die, I know of no action which I could take which would better declare to her people or the world the fact of her oppression and tyranny and of my valuation of liberty and also the fact that a life which is not free to follow its own inner light isn't worth living. Moreover, such a method of opposing oppression and tyranny would not damage any other personality as would the use of violence. And should a change in Germany eventually be wrought, as I firmly believe it would be, it would be because of a change of will towards the oppressed, because of the realization that her actions made life intolerable for men who meant her so little harm that they preferred to die themselves rather than by the use of violence against her attempt to sweep away her oppression and thereby further degrade the personalities of her people.

In a sense my present action is a blow for the sake of my own liberty, yet in a larger sense I am striking for the freedom of others who must come after me. My own chances of attaining liberty may be slim, yet I feel that if by my action even a few could be brought to see the evil of conscription, my life will not have been lived in vain. I have no fear that God will not reveal Himself to others, but I have a great fear that intolerance in the form of conscription may prevent them from serving Him as they believe He has called them to. For me to hesitate to strike at conscription with every means open to me, therefore, is for me to be false to the truth, false to the Master I profess to follow. As for war I feel there is room for an honest disagreement between men as to whether it is ever justifiable, but I cannot see how two men who profess to be dedicated to the truth should differ as to conscription, for freedom is the very first essential to the pursuit of truth.

CHARACTER "BAD"

In brief this is my stand. I do not see how I can retract unless more light comes to me.

August 25

It is shortly after 2:00 P.M. and you have doubtless finished one of those scrumptious Sunday dinners which we are always accustomed to have at home. Today marks the sixth day I have gone without a bite to eat and I am feeling as fit as a fiddle.

We are being watched pretty carefully by the regimental doctor here who, tho he does not agree with our main stand against war, is very sympathetic. He comes into the tent for quite a visit every morning. He seems somewhat surprised that we are bearing up so well, and even suspected that we had been eating a little. I guess if he has ever had dealings with starving men before, they have not been men who were starving for principle and needed only to say a word to get plenty to eat. When a man's spirit is in a job, you can't always calculate how he will act or what he can do or endure.

I hope Father does not consider coming on unless I send for him, for there is little that he can do here. I would advise him to act slowly if he desires to act at all. Above everything he must not do anything which would in any way compromise my stand against war or conscription. I am out for nothing short of absolute freedom. What the government will finally decide to do with us is of course the great question. Personally I should welcome a court-martial and dishonorable discharge. However, I am ready for the worst. I love life very dearly, but I love liberty more, and if I cannot have the latter I do not desire the former. I believe God is with me. Keep up your courage, Mother dear.

The episode of the hunger strike would have no place in these pages were the intention of the letters to draw a figure of heroic proportions. It was a mistake feverishly conceived and carried out in ignorance of and disregard for the tremendous difficulties which the government was facing. Its significance, however, lies not in the fact that it was an error which Gray later recognized and publicly acknowledged, but that it was one of the noncoöperative, nonviolent means tried by that small group of young men who in utter sincerity were willing to give their lives to call the attention of a hostile public to a social evil which to their minds was of paramount importance.

August 28

The ninth day of our hunger strike is drawing to a close, and I am still up and about, tho with greatly diminished energy. The truth is that it is much easier to sit than to stand and to lie than to sit. Tho my body is getting weaker, my abstinence from food does not seem to have affected my mind, which is as active as I ever knew it to be; it is fairly teeming with ideas and plans for the future.

Yesterday Evan was taken to the hospital because the doctor was beginning to get a little worried about him. We expected him back as the doctor said it was mainly for the purpose of examination that he was being taken, but he has not returned and the probability is they have begun forced feeding with him. Unless they come and get me I feel pretty sure by taking things easy I am good for several more days before being subjected to that painful process.

I do not believe the thought of food has ever occupied so large a place in my waking and sleeping dreams as it has the past week and more. It seems as if every trip I have ever taken anywhere was associated with plenty of good food. I just long to get home where I can eat some of Anna's[1] wonderful cooking. I wonder if I shall ever be able to again; at any rate I am getting great satisfaction from the hope.

I have practically made up my mind to go to agricultural college if I ever get free. As you know, my plans of reconstruction center around farming and the farm community which I hope to develop,[2] and I am convinced that the best preparation for the execution of my plans would be a thoro course in agriculture. Besides I long to learn about these things just for a personal satisfaction.

You have no idea how I hunger to get back to college, back to a regular life with lectures and books and even exams. For four months now I feel I have done nothing but degenerate in every way. It is well-nigh impossible to get anything done. Occasionally I get a book read, but it

[1] Anna was the beloved cook in the Gray household.
[2] This was a long-cherished ambition to the fulfillment of which he was later to give himself.

takes me four or five times as long to do it as it would ordinarily, and when I get thru I should hate to be quizzed as to its contents. The other men are all suffering from the same cause, inactivity and lack of privacy. I think if this kind of a life were to continue long, I would come out of imprisonment good for nothing.

On August 31st one of the officers at Fort Riley sent the following telegram to Gray's father:

Harold taken to hospital this morning. Felt well. No collapse.

Mrs. Thomas, mother of Evan Thomas, who had come on after Evan had been removed to the hospital, likewise telegraphed assuring Mr. Gray of the good treatment his son was receiving.

To these messages Mr. Gray replied to Harold.

We greatly appreciate —— and Mrs. Thomas's telegrams. Express our thanks to them. When I can be of service to you or you want to see me, let me know, and I will come immediately. You have carried your contention too far and you know I can't agree with you in your present stand, but I have done nothing to compromise you or injure your cause. You have certainly proved your sincerity. We are keenly interested in the outcome.

On September 1st, thirteen days after initiating his hunger strike, Gray wired his father as follows:

Thomas charged with defiance of government by refusing to eat. Believe Evan amply justified under conditions but as his refusal admits of possible unethical interpretation, I feel it advisable to abandon strike, waiting opportunity for defiance less open to misinterpretation. Receiving excellent treatment and feeling fine.

September 5

I am seated on one of the great big verandas of ward 6, section B, of the Base Hospital at Fort Riley. There is a fine cool breeze stirring, but the sun is slowly warming things up a bit. I am sitting in a fine big rocking chair, dressed in my pajamas, outdoor sleeping garment, and a white hospital wrapper. I have just had a wonderful breakfast, made my bed, and shaved, and am now feeling absolutely "top hole," being comfortable in body, mind, and soul. There is probably a good deal to write about, so I guess the best way is to try to follow some chronological order and begin at the beginning.

A week ago yesterday or today, I have forgotten which, two Y.M.C.A. secretaries came to my tent to pay me a visit. They had evidently come at Father's request. They burst into the tent with the apparent intention of taking me by storm. If I was very frank and said what I thought, it would be that I never ran across two more tactless, intolerant, empty-headed Y.M.C.A. secretaries in my life. They made no attempt whatever to get the facts regarding the cause of the hunger strike, which I take it was Father's purpose in having them visit me, but instead tried to show that I ought to be in this war, etc., etc. I put up with it for about fifteen minutes and told them I thought the argument was getting us nowhere, that I respected their views and only asked a similar respect for my own, upon which they got up and left, much to the great satisfaction of myself and tentmates, all of whom agreed these men were absolutely the limit.[1]

Saturday morning after a bitterly cold night I was awakened by the doctor and told that I was wanted up at headquarters. The news put more pep in me than I had had since the first day, and I fairly hustled about digging out my best clothes, shaving, etc., and was soon ready with Moore and Lunde to be driven up to headquarters.

At headquarters we were each interviewed separately by a major who had evidently been sent from Washington with instructions to get all the information regarding the conditions which had led up to the strike. It was entirely

---

[1] The report of this visit, telegraphed to a friend of Mr. Gray in Detroit, offers an interesting side light: "Have had interview young Gray. Find him very hard-headed and radical. He has listened to no argument nor can they do anything with him. Has been on hunger strike for ten days. Is not in danger however. Has been recommended for farm labor if he will accept. . . . Believe his father should see him if possible altho doubt if he could do any good."

[146]

a case of answering direct questions, which gave almost no chance to bring out the real underlying causes. The major was exceedingly courteous, as indeed all the officers and men have been who have had dealings with us since the strike began.

After the interviews we were taken back to the camp where we packed up a handful of belongings and were taken to the hospital. Almost the first people to greet us were Evan, Norman, and Mrs. Thomas. Evan, of course, was in bed, but very much alive just the same. I was pretty weak by this time and after a shower turned in.

About five in the afternoon I had my first forced feeding. I was taken into the ward kitchen and seated in a chair. A towel was put around my neck, my head was tilted back, and several orderlies and nurses proceeded to ram a long rubber tube down my throat. There was no pain, but an awful lot of gagging for I had not yet learned how to swallow a pipe line. When the red rubber tube had shortened its visible length by about a foot and a half or two feet, I was fed my supper which consisted of about a pint of milk poured into a funnel at the end of the tube not residing in my stomach. The whole procedure lasted only a few minutes. I had no trouble in keeping the milk down altho two pills shot it thru my system pretty fast during the night.

Sunday morning in the presence of all the orderlies and nurses of the ward, as well as a number of highly amused patients, I was fed my breakfast in a fashion similar to that of the night before, this time, however, the quantity of milk being increased and three eggs added. This time

the meal was a little too big and part of it came up. I
went back to bed all in.

Unfortunately Norman Thomas was called back to New
York about noon on Sunday, and I had only a short talk
with him before he left. He felt that the fact that we were
offering no resistance to the feeding relieved us of the
charge of suicide very greatly, altho he still felt it was not
the best course to take. His first-hand knowledge of the
conditions which had brought about the strike also helped
greatly to modify his opposition to the course we had
taken. He told me how my friends in New York viewed
the affair, and tho they did not know all the circumstances,
he felt their judgment was worth considering. He made
absolutely no attempt to change my attitude towards the
strike and urged me to be guided only by what I inwardly
felt to be right.

Sunday afternoon a colonel from headquarters came
over and interviewed Evan explaining to him what defiance meant and then ordered him in the name of the
U. S. to eat; this Evan refused to do, thus defying the U. S.
I was afraid that the colonel would come to me next, and
I frankly wanted time to think things over, for I saw that
whereas I was perfectly prepared to defy the U. S. in order
to get out of the army, even if it was to prison, I was not
sure whether I wanted to go before the country on a
charge of refusing to eat; people, who did not know the
cause, might confuse my action with an attempt to uphold
the right of suicide, which was the last thing I wanted to
do. Fortunately the colonel went away and left me alone
with my thoughts. When Mrs. Thomas came in a few

minutes later and learned what had happened, she was all broken up about it. She had hoped that Evan would come to see things differently and she felt strongly that everyone would interpret his action as upholding the right of suicide. In my own mind I felt that I could justify the course of action which I had taken on the grounds that the government had taken my body, which it would no longer permit me to use as I liked, and that it should therefore take care of it, I in the meantime offering neither to help nor hinder it in so doing.

The government persists in calling me a soldier, which I have repeatedly told them I would not be, and then it expects me to coöperate with it in keeping me a conscript, which I am unwilling to do for in a sense I am then responsible for my condition. Because the government offers me only two outlets for my energies, namely to become part of a vast organization whose sole aim is to prosecute a successful war or coöperate with it in keeping me a conscript, against both of which courses I am morally opposed, it punishes me with idleness, a vacant lot to live in, and raw rations to feed upon. Against such a status and such conditions I take the only effective way of protesting of which I know, a hunger strike.

The government policy in dealing with the C. O. problem is about as stupid as I can imagine. In Germany a C. O. is either shot, imprisoned, or discharged as "harmlessly insane." (A soldier, as the *Masses* once put it, I suppose being harmfully sane.) In England he is either imprisoned or freed as being sincere, but in the U. S. they persist in trying to make a soldier of him, address him as private and keep him under the military, and because he will not coöperate with them in this course of action, even to the extent of cooking his own meals, they subject him to treatment or conditions as bad if not worse than prison and still persist in telling him he is not a prisoner, but a soldier, which he would rather die than be.

After supper Sunday evening I had a long talk with Evan which ended in my sending Father the telegram. If I were rewriting it, I think I should substitute some other word for "opportunity" in "I feel it advisable to abandon strike, awaiting opportunity for defiance less open to misinterpretation." It makes it look too much as if I wanted to defy the government, which, of course, is not the case. I simply mean that if she persists in holding me as a soldier and calling me one, it will be a relief when she orders me to do something which my refusing to do will land me in prison.

Monday morning I ate my breakfast in bed and thus wiggled my jaws for the first time in two weeks, lacking a few hours. After breakfast Lunde and I sent a joint telegram to Baker: "Possibility of our action in hunger strike for liberty leading to unethical interpretation causes us to abandon it."

On Tuesday, September 3rd, we were visited by a major, I think from Washington, who had evidently been sent on to try and break up the strike by persuasion. Evan had a long siege with him first and then my turn came. There were two other majors present. The interview was one of the most interesting I have had and lasted a good while.

The major is in the medical corps and evidently quite a noted psychologist. He certainly made me hump some. He is a Harvard man and we were soon on the most friendly terms. But if his aim was to get me into the army, or to persuade me to accept a farm furlough, or even for that matter to work in prison, I fear he failed most lamentably. I have lots of fun with these men because I usually grant so much to them, but keep as my stronghold the fact that I cannot see it their way in spite of all the arguments against me and until I can see it I intend to live by the highest light that I have. Until I am no longer able to fight, I simply will not accept the world as I find it, no matter what price I have to pay.

As the major says, there is only a little handful of men of intelligence and training among the C. O.'s, but because we are so persistent on the issue of conscription and freedom of conscience we present a very real problem to the government. In a war for democracy it is hardly good policy to punish men for having a conscience, for an autocracy like Germany can do that quite as well as a democracy.

Monday morning, September 2nd, I received Father's wonderful telegram. Seldom has anything made me so happy. If ever a man had reason to be thankful for the family he was born into, I am that man. I showed the telegram to Evan and he agreed I certainly had a wonderful father. I really wanted to have you both in the worst kind of way, but I knew it would be dreadfully selfish of me to ask you. There was nothing you could do and everything was going beautifully. Before I broke the strike, I was in hopes you would come on in response to Mrs. Thomas's telegram, but now of course I am glad you did not do so. I guess I owe a great deal more to your prayers these few weeks than I can ever realize. Believe me, I sure am grateful. Altho I am not proud of my behavior, I am not exactly ashamed of it. I tried to do what I felt was right. The experience has helped me a great deal. I have had to do a lot of thinking and I guess that never does any harm. I can speak now of a hunger strike and its ethics with something of first-hand knowledge.

Evan and Moore have now both begun to eat, but both have stated that they will instantly go on strike again if returned to the old conditions. The major practically assured them that this would not happen. Whether or not I shall ever employ the hunger strike again, I am not prepared to say definitely. On the whole I am averse to its use.

Altho I am beginning to feel as fit as ever, there is a good prospect of our remaining in the hospital for some time to come. There are eleven of us altogether who were brought here during the last couple of days of the strike. There were twenty who struck in all, altho only four of us were out for liberation from the whole business; the others were striking only for prepared food. Altho the government has not changed, other C.O.'s have consented to do the cooking and things are apparently running smoothly.

Yesterday it was pretty cold here, and the captain who is in charge of our ward sent me down to the tents to get warm underwear for the others here. It was dreary and cold down there and I sure was thankful I had a building to live in instead of tents.

It has been great being here at the hospital with a real bed with white sheets to sleep in, with rocking chairs to sit in, no flies, and hot water to wash with. Everybody is just as nice as can be. At first the captain thought he could break us and I understand he even applied for the job, but I guess he has changed his mind since. He may not agree with us, but I guess he respects us now as do all his staff, apparently.

They evidently intend to turn us out of the hospital in better condition than we ever were in before in our lives. Day before yesterday we had a blood test taken and we have all been carefully examined for latent troubles. I lost twenty pounds during the two weeks' fast, but I am putting it on now more quickly than I lost it. You ought to see me eat. I don't think I ever ate so much in my life, and still it seems as if I got up from the table hungrier than when I sat down. We are having splendid grub which sure is some relief after the food and cooking we had to put up with at the tent colony.

If you only knew how often I think of you all and how very, very much I love you. I wonder if the war will ever end and let me come home again, but then how many million are wondering the same thing!

In a letter to his mother, dated September 7th, Gray reviewed the events leading up to the hunger strike, events already made clear in his earlier letters, and explained more fully his reasons for abandoning it.

September 7

It is a week today since I came here to the hospital and I am now fatter than almost ever before and I think every bit as healthy. I am eating perfectly huge meals; I sit in the open most of the day in a rocker and read, and take an hour off between four and five in the afternoons for calisthenics and a shower. I am sleeping like a top. Such is my physical condition.

At first I entered upon this strike with a view only to obtaining prepared food. But to use a hunger strike merely to try to force the government to give me cooked food, when what I really wanted was my liberty, seemed so small that when on October 21st Howard Moore stated his determination not to eat until set free, I readily fell into line. It seemed the thing to do and I did it without a great deal of consideration as to the ethics of the course of action I was entering upon.

For ten days every argument which came to my mind seemed to favor the course I had taken, and then suddenly I began to have doubts. I began to realize that if the government did not set me free or feed me forcefully, an overt act on my part was involved which would make me in a sense responsible for my own death. I was perfectly ready to die provided others took my life because of my refusal to make a moral compromise, but I was not ready to take my own life.

Haunted by many misgivings I was sent to the hospital

[154]

at the end of the twelfth day of fasting. Sunday afternoon, September 1st, things came to a sudden crisis when Evan was confronted with the choice of eating or defying the U. S. government, in the person of a colonel, and chose the latter course. This meant that if he was court-martialed, the specific charge laid him open to a serious misinterpretation of motive. Personally I was not at all prepared for this. It put a face on things which I did not like at all. I began to see that I had made a mistake and the manly thing to do was to admit it and back down. Accordingly that night I received my third and last forced feeding, after which I wired home that I was abandoning the strike; then I went and had a talk with the captain who was in charge of our ward. I had been wrong, my mistake had caused him a lot of worry and trouble, and I wanted to apologize. He was very nice and heartily accepted my apology. I left his office with a tremendous load lifted from my mind.

If it is true that we sometimes profit quite as much by our mistakes as by our successes, there is little doubt that I am a wiser man today than I was three weeks ago. I am done with hunger strikes once and for all, for I believe I have no more right to gamble with my health than to gamble with my life. I have had to do some hard thinking and it has not hurt me. I have registered a protest against the government's policy in dealing with me, but its value is very doubtful. It is not a comforting thought to feel that you have made a fool of yourself in the eyes of yourself and friends. Will you people at home ever be able to forgive me for the worry I have caused you by my mad behavior? I shall try to be more careful next time for your sakes. . . . You will not forget to pray that I may be guided into doing the right thing, will you?

Junction City Library
September 14

As you can see by the above I am in Junction City. Quite unexpectedly on Thursday we were discharged from the hospital and taken back to our old stand in the field. We had practically been assured that we would not be sent back there; hence the surprise. We were all in splendid condition, however, so I suppose they could find no valid reason for keeping us longer. Things at present are in a decidedly unsatisfactory state, and our one hope is that the situation is only a temporary one and that some move will be made in the next day or two.

When ten of us who had been living at the hospital got back to camp, we found that most of the men were doing K.P. work and were cooking not only for themselves but for those "who would not even do non-combatant work to the extent of cooking their own meals." (This is quoted from a government report.) We had three meals with the crowd and then there began to be trouble again. Very naturally some of the men balked at cooking for a lot of men who would not work. A meeting was held and altho it was voted to continue preparing the meals for the whole camp, the arrangement doesn't suit anybody.

Thomas, Moore, Lunde, and I felt so strongly that we did not care to sponge on these men who were willing to cook for us but to whom we were, nevertheless, a thorn in the flesh that we decided to take the raw rations and eat what we could of them. But you can easily see that this is unsatisfactory. If things are not altered by Monday, Moore and Thomas will again go on a hunger strike, but Lunde and I cannot see our way clear to doing this again, for reasons which I have already written you. If, on the other hand, there is nothing doing in the course of the next couple of days, we are frankly up against it. I am not yet ready to desert, I cannot conscientiously coöperate with the government in keeping me a soldier, I hate to sponge on other men, and I cannot keep fit for long on raw rations. Of course the rations which are issued contain some things such as bread and some canned things which can be eaten without cooking, but even then I question whether a man could keep fit any length of time on such a diet. In short the government has me up against a wall. It is going to try to force me either to take some step which will land me in prison or to be a good little boy and help it keep me a soldier. What I shall probably do will be to accept the hospitality of the other men who have offered to cook for me.

There are many rumors to the effect that we are soon to be sent back to Leavenworth, but there is nothing definite as yet.

Do not bother any more about Drummond's book or about sending on *Foundations*. I should like Emerson's *Essays*, however, and likewise Tolstoi, particularly *My Religion* and *What Must We Do?* or some such title.

I am sorry you were led to feel that the humdrum things of life did not appeal to me. I only wish to goodness I could get back to humdrum things for a little while and away from this war and its problems. I wish you would write more news about the family and what goes on at home. That is just the sort of thing I want. I get quite enough of the other here.

I wish you were here now to talk to instead of in Detroit. If we could only have a good talk, I think the world would look brighter. I guess I am having a genuine attack of the blues today and this letter shows it. You must forgive me for attempting to write when I am in such a mood. Remember they don't as a rule last long. Tomorrow I shall feel better.

September 21

I am sitting on my bunk in our old lot with my suitcase beside me all packed ready to go to the guardhouse. Sixty-two of the C.O.'s have already been taken and the thirty-odd of us who remain are sitting around in little groups awaiting our turn to be called. But I am ahead of my story and had better go back a bit.

Last Saturday, a week ago, I paid a visit to Junction City and returned a pretty discouraged man. I had carried one policy to its logical conclusion, the hunger strike, and had thereby proved it to be a bad one; I was at a loss to know what course to pursue next. That morning I had eaten what raw rations I could for breakfast and at noon I had done the same, but the arrangement was distinctly unsatisfactory from both a mental and a physical point of view.

For some time now, in fact, since the very first, the camp in which we live has gone unpoliced, and it has become very unsanitary. Altho we have never been ordered directly to police up the grounds, the colonel claimed that in not doing so we had been defiant. He then read the President's proclamation regarding C.O.'s being assigned to noncombatant work and told us he would give us till the next day to make up our minds.

Tuesday afternoon we were again assembled, and after refusing noncombatant work in a body the colonel proceeded to take-eight men, previously selected, and ordered them one by one to shovel a pile of refuse from our kitchen into a wagon to be hauled away. All eight of the men refused and were ordered to pack up their things. In a few minutes they were off for the guardhouse. How on earth I happened not to be called I do not know, for both Moore and Lunde were among the first. They refused on the basis that they could not obey a military command.

When it was all over, I gave a sigh of relief for frankly I was up in the air and for a while I do not know what I should have done. I should probably have refused and gone with the others. I wanted time to think it over. Here was a case too much like that of the refusal to eat. We had obviously made the pile of débris and it could easily be interpreted as being a menace to our health. To refuse to remove it could, therefore, be interpreted as refusal to "keep ourselves and our surroundings clean."

Tuesday evening I went for a walk and for the first time in weeks got alone where I could think things over and pray. In the crowded surroundings of the camp and hospital I have found it very, very difficult really to pray and try to look at things in their proper perspective. The moon was bright, the air clear and cool, and as I walked along a deserted road, I did the first real praying I have succeeded in doing in a long time, and somehow things began to clear themselves.

I finally came to the conclusion that it not only was not wrong to do my own cooking and cleaning and such other work as pertained only to my own upkeep, but that I would be wrong in refusing to do these things, provided the President in a proclamation commanded me to. His proclamation of July 30th stated that I would be expected to look after myself to the extent of cooking my own food and keeping myself and my quarters clean.

The second question was whether I ought to obey a military command at all, even when commanded to do something which I could not only conscientiously do, but would do anyway if left to myself. As a matter of fact I had obeyed a military command when I voluntarily went to camp, and this I would not have done if left to myself and not ordered to report.

The question is one which goes far beyond the problem of compulsory service and raises the whole question as to whether the state has any right to force people to do anything, a right which, if denied, means philosophical anarchy. Altho Judge Stone once accused me of being a philosophical anarchist, I do not believe I am open to that charge. I believe, for example, that the state has the right to enforce sanitary and health regulations, to imprison criminals for the purpose of reforming them, and even to conscript capital in the form of taxes in order to run institutions and make improvements for the common good.

But such functions of the state are very different from demanding compulsory services from men. The state is primarily a material institution. It exists for the purpose of protecting and improving the material wealth, of seeing that justice is done between man and man as regards material things. Therefore, if a man wishes to spend his life in the accumulation of material wealth and this accumulation is dependent upon the state both thru its protective power and its public facilities, I believe the state has the right thru taxation to demand, and if resisted, thru confiscation, forcefully to compel the payment of taxes. But if a man is not concerned with material wealth, why on earth should he be compelled to be, by being forced to give his life or time in work for its accumulation or protection, which is the case in "work or fight"? And if a man who is not concerned with material things ought not to be compelled to accumulate or protect them, certainly a man who believes that they ought not to be accumulated or protected at the expense of spiritual things ought not to be compelled to protect or accumulate them.

In a recent note Roger Baldwin spoke of the hunger strike as an "impatient offensive" and the phrase is a most descriptive one. As I look back at the hunger strike now I am almost at a loss to account for the fact of my so far abandoning my principles of nonresistance as to adopt it.

In ordering me to remove débris, which I had helped to create, or to keep clean the area or buildings in which I live or which I use, I believe the state is acting within its rights because to refuse to do these things would make me responsible for menacing the health of myself and others. To refuse to keep myself and my surroundings clean might seem to deny the right of the government even to enforce sanitary regulations, which is by no means what I am fighting against, but rather I am fighting against the right of the government to make me work for it. Therefore, by waiting until I had an order to do something which had no direct bearing upon my own care or my share of the care of such area, buildings or equipment as I use and deem necessary to my well-being, and then refusing to obey, there could be less doubt as to what it was I was opposing.

On Wednesday the procedure of the previous day was repeated. We were all lined up and the colonel ordered eight men in turn to clean up the pile of débris back of the kitchen. Seven of them refused and another was called from the main group who likewise refused, making eight in all who were promptly dispatched to the guardhouse. We were then dismissed till the next day when the performance was repeated; this time of some fifty-one men all but seven refused to comply with the colonel's order. I was among the last called and obeyed without hesitation.

Friday I did K.P. work in our out-of-door kitchen and spent about the happiest day I have spent in a long time. I cleaned up everything in sight, rearranged things to suit my fancy, and ended the day by building some seats for a kitchen table. It was great to be able just to let myself go and work and at the same time have no conscientious scruples about doing it. If the government is determined not to let us go free, how I wish they would intern us and let us have our own workshops, educational classes, the same as interned aliens have, but I suppose that would make it so easy for C.O.'s that a few who might otherwise become soldiers would join us; therefore, we must be kept in constant uncertainty with regard to the future with a twenty years sentence in the D.B.'s constantly hanging over our heads. You see why any study or concentration on problems other than those which immediately confront us is well-nigh impossible.

I started to write this letter on Saturday. It is now Monday and I am still not in the guardhouse as I fully expected to be. The reason I expected to go was that four of our number were ordered to cut the grass outside the official boundaries of our lot and refused, as did eight others who were later called up. All twelve were sent to the guardhouse and the rest of us all hastened to pack our things awaiting our turn to be called out, but the lieutenant seemed to think twelve men were enough for one day and none of the rest of us were called.

Saturday afternoon I got a pass to Junction City where I had a nice chicken dinner and went to the movies.

This morning everybody expected something to happen and the first thing we did was to get things packed ready to move to the guardhouse. On Saturday the guard who walks the boundaries of our camp began to include within our boundaries an area of land which we never have used, which was not needed at all and which is used by the military for storing firewood and carts belonging to the Q.M.C. It was obviously a trick to get us to clean it and cut the weeds, on the ground that it was part of our camp, treating our refusal to do it as a refusal to police our own grounds. Every man in camp was determined to go to the guardhouse rather than do the work. When there were eighty or more of us, our lot was judged by the military to be plenty large enough for us, and in a General Order No. 85 of September 17th signed by the colonel himself these boundaries were given. Now several days later when there are only some thirty of us left in camp and the government is determined by hook or crook to make us work, they apparently suddenly find it necessary to enlarge our boundaries, a process which could go on indefinitely. But today has passed and we have not yet been ordered to clean beyond the old limits; instead, things seem to have taken another and a more favorable turn.

A definite daily program has been posted by the military which provides for ordinary duties about the camp such as furling tents, raking the grounds, cleaning the latrines, etc., and then provides for long hikes to take the place of drilling and the other duties of a soldier. This means two long hikes a day ending at 4:00 P.M., with roll call at 5:05 and the rest of the day to ourselves. Provided we are not ordered to march in military formation, which we certainly were not this afternoon when we took our first hike, or otherwise ordered to abide by military formalities which would give us the appearance of being soldiers, I think things will run along very nicely unless the military tries to spring something new on us.

I hope my present stand in the face of all your arguments and everything has not given you the impression that I am pig-headed and want to do everything by myself and do not care for the advice and help of others. If it has, it has given you a very wrong impression.

If you are considering coming on at all, I think you had better not delay in the hope that things will settle down here. Even if I am sent to the guardhouse, I think you would have no difficulties in procuring passes to see me for a short time every day anyway, and I am, oh, so keen to see you both! I only wish the whole family could come with you.

I wish that you would bring my scale ruler with you. Later on if we should settle down to something resembling a life of internment, I may have you send on my whole drawing set. I have a friend, an architect and a graduate of Columbia, who has kindly volunteered to coach me in house-planning and drawing if we can ever be assured of any peace. I have some great ideas for a new house.

Altho at times I grow impatient and long to be free again, I do not think this experience here is doing me any harm. As we often remark among ourselves, it is really equal to a college education. We certainly have to do a lot of thinking on problems which may involve us in a twenty years sentence any moment. If my letters are unduly filled with a discussion of these problems, you must forgive me.

> Base Hospital, Fort Riley
> Cell 20 Guardhouse
> Fort Riley, Kansas
> *October 6*

As you can gather from the above addresses things have

been moving since I last wrote. On Saturday, September 28th, all of the thirty-odd men still residing in our C.O. tent colony were marched up to the old barracks, from whence together with the other C.O.'s from the barracks we were marched to the guardhouse. There in the court-yard we were all lined up, a bundle of rakes was produced, and one by one we were ordered to take one in order to rake up "anywhere we were ordered within the post, prob-ably the parade grounds." All but three of the colony men refused without hesitation, as well as several of the gov-ernment's "good C.O.'s"[1] from the barracks. This proce-dure over with, we packed up for the last time and then we were off to the guardhouse. At the guardhouse we were searched and everything was taken from us except the clothes we had on, extra socks and underwear, hairbrushes, toothbrush, soap, towel, and Bible. We were also left our blankets under the guise of which I smuggled in my cape. Then we were escorted to two large cells in the basement where we were literally packed in like sardines. There were forty-two in my cell.

The cells were certainly not over thirty-five by forty feet. On two sides there was a solid wall, but on the third, bars constituted a barrier. The floor was of cement. Save in the latrine and cell opposite near the stairs there were no win-dows whatever in our part of the basement. All our light and air, what little of both we had, came from above, thru a two-foot air space which separated the floor above

---

[1] The "good C.O.'s" were those who upon arrival at Fort Riley had ex-pressed their willingness to do K.P. duty for the entire barracks; they had never been moved to the tent colony.

from the main walls of the building. Fortunately we were furnished with comfortable double-decked beds.

When we were put in the guardhouse, I think it was the intention of those who put us there to try us out until Monday when we would be given another order to work; if we refused that, we would go on bread and water. But the only change which took place on Monday was that twelve of the men from the cell I was in were placed next door; this gave us more room to stretch in. The reason for this failure of the authorities to follow things up apparently seems to have been an order from G.H.Q. to feed all men well on account of danger of influenza. That left the government with no adequate punishment to give us if we had refused, as all of us would have done, had we been ordered to work again on Monday.

Altho penned in a cell from Saturday night till Friday morning, when I was taken to the hospital with influenza, and only allowed out when the Corporal of the Keys chose to let us visit the latrine or march us upstairs for meals, the time passed rapidly and gaily. We sang from morning till night and the singing was caused by anything but an attempt to keep up our spirits. We were just plain happy and it had to come out.

It was good to see the other men again, the ones who had preceded us to the guardhouse. Altho both Evan and Lunde were in solitary, I saw quite a little of them at odd moments.

The main hardships were the absence of writing materials or reading matter except our Bibles, poor light and air, and the difficulty of always getting to the latrine when

[167]

one wanted to. But as I have said I was pretty happy inside at getting to prison on so clear an issue as refusal to rake the parade grounds, which had nothing whatever to do with the case of our tent colony or of ourselves. Incidentally the men from the barracks who did take the rakes on Saturday have been kept working every day since and have now been organized into the 425th Labor Battalion.

On Wednesday we were given our shaving articles, and Friday we had been promised a sheet of writing paper apiece and our pens. I had intended writing you on Sunday the 29th before I was sent to the guardhouse, and as this was only the day after I was sent there and we were not allowed to write till Friday, it made a bit longer gap between letters than I should have liked.

Thursday night, however, I came down with influenza; that knocked all hopes of writing the following day. During the night, a most dreadfully long one, I had a chill and the most severe ache in my back and legs. My temperature, however, was not high, only a little over 100 degrees, as registered in the morning. For two days past men had been coming down with influenza.

Friday, Saturday, and Sunday were pretty miserable days. I came down with a cold, my fever kept over 100, and my back and head ached. Sunday I got this stationery from a "Y" man passing thru the ward and started this letter with another fellow's pencil, but I had to give it up halfway down the first sheet. On Monday morning I collapsed in the latrine and had to be carried back to bed. That was the worst day of all. When one of the "Y" men came thru the ward that night, I asked him to wire Father, "In the hospital with influenza, no cause for worry, writing soon." I thought you ought to know and I didn't know when I might get to write; besides, I think I just hoped you might decide to come on and I wanted to see you pretty bad. This is the first time I think I have ever been sick away from home and it isn't easy. It is lots nicer where there is a mother within hailing distance.

But yesterday I began to feel something like my old self again and today the same. My temperature is almost normal, my cold is breaking, and my back hardly aches at all any more.

The papers make interesting reading these days, don't they? I think Wilson has made a master stroke in sending the note he has to Germany. I shall be disappointed if Germany does not give in on every point, for to refuse will put her rulers in a bad way with the people. I think the prospects of peace within a few months are brighter than I have ever known them. However, I am not unduly optimistic or building any false hopes on an early release from prison or the army.

From actual experience I am learning of the tremendous power of nonresistance, a game in which patience is the biggest factor. If the government can get us impatient and make us go on the aggressive, it has us either for desertion or defiance; but when we keep patient, do our own work or profess a willingness to and yet courteously but firmly refuse to give an inch, every time we are ordered across the line, well, the government, I think, is clearly stumped to know how to deal with us. As yet, tho eleven days have passed since I became a prisoner, no charges have been read to me nor is there mention of a court-martial. According to law we are not supposed to be held more than eight days unless charges are read to us. The men who preceded us to the guardhouse, with the exception of Thomas, all were charged with defiance and are awaiting trial. It is all rather a queer performance. However, as always, I am ready for whatever comes.

October 13

As I write the sun shines thru the bars of my cell and falls across the paper. I am out of the hospital now and back at the guardhouse, but this time in much more comfortable circumstances. Instead of being down in the basement I am in "solitary" on the ground floor. My cell seven by five feet faces the west and is opposite a long window which admits plenty of light and air. In the late afternoon and evening I get the sun and can see it set.

My cell is absolutely barren save for an iron latticework bed which hinges against the long side of the cell. The mattress of the bed as well as the blankets has to be taken out every morning for a sunning, and as we don't go out after them until nearly dark, this means that we have only the bare iron slats to sit on all day. However, it is a very slight hardship. When my bed is folded against the wall, it gives me quite a little room for exercise of the standing variety.

It is rather hard being without any writing material or

anything except my Bible to read. It may be a good thing, however, as it will force me to make the acquaintance of the book about which I am ashamed to say I am at present woefully in ignorance. I have already nearly finished Genesis.

I got out of the hospital Friday night feeling well indeed. When I got back to the guardhouse, I found things going along as usual. Two large fat letters, probably from you, had come for me during my absence and had been held until that day when they had been forwarded to me at the hospital. They have not been returned. I fear there is slim chance of my ever seeing them. I wish you would write as often as you can find time as letters are among the few things we are allowed to receive and take to our cells. By the way, will you dispatch immediately parcel post two cakes of Palmolive face soap and one bar of P. & G. laundry soap. My supply of soap is running low, and if you can send me a little it will save no end of trouble here, for of course I am not able to get out and make purchases myself.

At present I am only allowed one letter a week and I think by all rights that belongs to you.

By the strange ways in which rumors and news get into the guardhouse we have learned today of Germany's reply to the president's three questions. Things surely look hopeful. The spirits of the men are running high here. Everybody is hoping that somehow our release may come with peace and that both may come as speedily as possible. I dare not express my own wishes. I am so anxious to have this whole business over with. I think when I do get out, I shall make a bee line for 116[1] and stay there for a while. Home will never have looked so good to me. It will be simply wonderful to see you and Father again. It seems like a perfect age since July 4th when we last parted. Wouldn't it be great if we could all spend Christmas together? My freedom would certainly be the greatest present the state could give me.

Evan Thomas is on the same floor with me now, and as all the C.O.'s on this floor eat together I see him every meal. He was court-martialed while I was at the hospital but he has not yet received his sentence. While I was in the hospital, the other men received their charges; they were also told that they would probably never be tried. That may mean that in the event of peace they will all be discharged instead. I have not had my charges read to me, but I presume they are the same as the others.

Erling Lunde and several of my other friends are in solitary either below me or right near-by on the same floor. We talk to each other a good deal and even occasionally try to sing together. The men in the big cell downstairs are singing together now and from a distance it sounds fine.

I am eating at the first of three tables and the food is very good, indeed, considering where we are. I am sleeping fine and if we are released in the course of the next month or two, I ought to come home in good physical condition. However, I dare say I have been living under a greater

[1] The house number of the Gray home in Detroit.

strain the last few months than I realize, and a good rest and change will be tremendously welcomed.

The letter of October 20th is addressed to his older sister.

October 20

It is surprising to me how quickly I have gotten used to this place and to solitary. Altho I have never suffered here, the first few days were a bit hard, but now I am really enjoying myself. I have plenty of warm clothes, a good bed, and plenty of good wholesome food. For about an hour or so every day we are allowed out of our cells, in order to clean them out with a hose and to exercise by walking around the balcony just outside our cells. After the months of confinement with other men, the privacy of solitary is a tremendous blessing. I am memorizing the Gospel of Mark as translated by Weymouth. It is remarkable how unthought-of meaning comes with the careful reading necessary to memorizing. I am getting a chance, too, to pray. Deprived once more of human companionship, as in England, I am finding myself thrown back on God, or I think I should better say, getting still, I am able to enjoy God's companionship and it is a joy. I think we form our deepest friendships with those who share with us the deepest experiences of life. As I come to learn what it is like to be rejected of men, I somehow feel I am sharing with God in a very common experience of His life, and the bonds of friendship are thus strengthened.

Thank you so much for the poetry. It is all beautiful.

[173]

The poems by Barbauld and George Eliot are new and I shall memorize them; the one by Edward Sill is one I have learned before, but am very glad to have here. Sill, you may know, was an Exeter man, and one of the alumni of whom we are very proud.

I am feeling very well again in spite of my influenza; still I should certainly love to sit with you for a while in the sun and now and again drink one of those delicious albumens of Anna's. I wonder how long I must wait before I visit 116 again. What a beautiful little house it is and what dear wonderful people live in it!

October 27

Father's first letter with the poetry reached me in my little cell No. 9 last Monday, and his second letter was delivered to me on Thursday in my new palatial apartment. For on Thursday of last week, quite to my surprise, the lieutenant in charge here asked me if I would like to move into the big cell which was formerly occupied by Evan Thomas. Evan has now been sent to Fort Leavenworth with a number of others. He was sentenced to life imprisonment at hard labor, but owing to the clemency of General Wood at Camp Funston his sentence was reduced to twenty-five years. His cell, which now I occupy in company with five others, is the prize cell of the place. The main room, which is about fourteen by twenty feet, is bounded on one side by the outside wall of the building; this wall contains two large windows which face the west and open out of a court below and a mule stable beyond, with a glimpse of the river from one window and the main road from the other. The room contains three double-deck iron beds with comfortable springs and mattresses, a writing desk, and boxes in which to keep our clothes. Adjoining the main room and with free access to it is a good-sized latrine.

I have my five companions. . . . More by chance than anything else the six of us eat together at a separate table in the dining room. We are getting good service and more than enough to eat of excellent food. Taken all in all I am more comfortable physically than I have been at any time since April 26th when I was drafted, and I certainly never was so happy. My only care is for you and Father who, I fear, are not at all reconciled to my stand. How I wish I could live the truth as I see it and please you both at the same time, but it seems to be impossible and I simply cannot surrender my self-respect by living a lie, living as if I believed in war and conscription when I do not. The last thing I want to do is to oppose my government, and I am not here to protest against the policy which they have adopted in dealing with Germany, but only because they have ordered me to take part in something I do not and cannot believe in.

Last week I received my charges; I shall probably be court-martialed some day this week. The charges read: "In that Private Harold S. Gray, Co. A 1st Casual Bat., Conscientious Objectors, Fort Riley, Kansas, having received a lawful command from 1st Lieut. James D. Carter, his superior officer, to assist in policing up the parade grounds, did on or about the 28th day of September, 1918, willfully disobey the same." I am exceedingly well pleased with the wording of my charge as it leaves no possible room for misinterpretation, as would have been the case if in the hospital I had been ordered to eat and had refused. Policing the parade grounds is a soldier's work pure and simple.

Thanks to the lieutenant I have been allowed paper and pencil with which to work on a statement of my case to be presented to the court in defense of my action. I have never really drawn up a statement of what I believe and I am trying hard to make this one as thoro and clear as possible. Aside from turning in a brief statement, most of the men are making no effort to defend themselves. If the government thinks the best place for us is in prison, what we may say at a court-martial can make little or no difference. I find that in rethinking my position many new points are coming out which I had not observed before. The solitary helped me a lot in this regard. Indeed it was more a blessing than anything else. In a way I almost miss it, but fortunately my companions are fairly quiet so that I have a good deal of time to myself in which to think. I am having difficulty expressing myself as clearly as I should like. I guess I have grown rusty at the job.

For the time being, until my court-martial is over, I have stopped my memorizing of the Gospel of Mark. I was very pleased with some of the poems Father sent me and memorized a couple of them and would have memorized more had my thoughts not been forced into other channels. I shall probably have plenty of time for memorizing at Fort Leavenworth. As I see things at present, if

I am ordered in the D. B.[1] to do military work such as keeping the post policed, or in fact ordered to do any work that is in support of the military, as I understand practically all of the work is, I shall be forced to refuse to work and take the penalty. If, however, the work is strictly civil and has no bearing on the military, that is, there is nothing wrong in it *per se*, I think I shall do it. To do such work under conscription outside of prison would look as if I condoned conscription, but this possibility is removed when, having been sent to prison for the very reason that I will not condone conscription, I am forced to work there. I do not feel that I would then be living a lie or surrendering my self-respect as would be the case outside of prison. My only hope is that the government will make some special arrangement for imprisoning C.O.'s, so that we can conscientiously work. If they do not, it is likely to go hard with us.

Thanks for the soap you sent, which arrived last Wednesday. I have been on the point of writing for two suits of my heavy underwear, but the steam has now been turned on, and it is so comfortable that I think I shall have you hold them for the time being.

November 3

The big event is at last a thing of the past. Last Thursday, the 31st of October, I was court-martialed at Camp Funston, Kansas. Up till last Tuesday I worked pretty hard on my statement and then I began to see that it was much too long and I was by no means thru, so Wednes-

[1] Disciplinary Barracks.

day I wrote a much briefer statement which really covered every essential point. I barely had time to brush it up and copy it on Thursday when I was called out shortly after dinner, along with seven others, and conducted to Funston in a big auto truck. There I was the second of the group to be tried.

The trial took place in a large room about the size of our mess hall at Custer. In the center of the room were a dozen or fourteen tables, each large enough for one man to write at and all arranged in a circle. At seven of the tables sat my judges, all majors or captains; at another sat the Judge Advocate, then the prosecuting attorney, next the witnesses against me, then the court stenographer and next to him was my table.

After the court had been sworn in and numerous articles read for my benefit and that of the court, the witnesses were called in who testified against me and finally I was asked if I had anything to say. I told the president of the court that I had written out a statement which I would read or turn in as an exhibit, as the court desired. The president asked that I read it, which I did. I never felt more cool or collected and I read my statement slowly and clearly. I am going to enclose a copy of the statement in this letter in the hopes that the censor will pass it. In order to bring out my beliefs regarding war and compulsory service I wrote the statement in the form of a history of my experience as a C.O. Either the Judge Advocate had had my record thoroly examined by the Department of Justice and as a result believed that I should be given a stiff sentence, which is the more reasonable explanation, or else he interpreted my statement as an attempt to prove my own sincerity, which was the last thought in my mind when I wrote it, for when I had finished he rose to his feet and urged that I be given the death sentence for cowardice. When the Judge Advocate had concluded his remarks with a grand flourish, the president of the court asked if I had anything further to say in my defense. I thanked him, but said I had nothing further to say, whereupon the trial came to a conclusion.

So far as I am able to learn Thomas and I are the only men for whom the death sentence has been asked, and since Thomas received twenty-five years' hard labor at Fort Leavenworth, my fate will probably be the same. However, if they should give me the death sentence and it should be approved by Washington, I know of no one who is more ready to die for a great cause than I am, and I certainly know of no greater cause than that of upholding the majesty and freedom of conscience.

Speaking of death, on Thursday I received Evelyn's wonderful letter shortly before being called to Funston. I did not have time to finish it before my trial and I left the poem to read afterwards. When I came out of the court room, I pulled the letter out to read the poetry. The poem was Browning's "Prospice" so that the first words which struck my eye were: "Fear death? to feel the fog in my throat." I wonder if Evelyn thought when she wrote it that it would be the first thing I would read after a court-martial in which it had been strongly urged that I be given the death penalty.

I am being excellently treated here and never was in

better health. I am eating huge meals, leading the others in the Exeter drill, which takes nearly one-half hour daily, and am sleeping like a top. The Lord is very near and our cell is a very, very happy place.

Harold Gray's Statement before the Court-Martial

Honorable Gentlemen of the Court-Martial, I have been brought before you today charged with the willful disobedience of a lawful military command. On September 28, 1918, I was ordered to assist in policing up the parade grounds at Fort Riley, Kansas, and refused. In the following statement, which I offer to this court for consideration, I have tried to set forth briefly the grounds for this refusal.

The history of my present stand as a conscientious objector to war and compulsory service begins with the spring of 1916 when as an undergraduate at Harvard University I volunteered for Y.M.C.A. service among Allied troops and German prisoners of war in England. Owing to past experience in Christian work, both as president of the Christian Association at Phillips Exeter Academy and as head of the Freshmen Bible work at Harvard, where I was later also elected president of the Christian Association, my services were accepted. For sixteen months, from July, 1916, to December, 1917, I was engaged in war work in England under the auspices of the International Committee of the Y.M.C.A.

It was in England that I first came to consider seriously the problem of war. I had gone to England, accepting

without question the common conception of the cause of
this war, namely that of a war-mad, criminal nation suddenly attacking her innocent neighbors, and I was in complete accord with the Allies' method of dealing with those
causes.

Thru contact with the men of both sides in this conflict
I was afforded an unusual opportunity for study and observation, with the result that I early came to see that what
I had supposed to be the war's underlying cause, namely
the materialistic ambitions of the rulers of Germany, was
in reality only its immediate cause and that the fundamental cause lay in the present, unchristian, materialistic social order in which we live, a social order with sin in the
human heart as its source and war as its logical and inevitable outcome. The belief that sin can be overthrown or
even checked by a scientific butchering of the flower of
the world's manhood was one which I could not accept. I
saw that what was needed was a regeneration of men's
hearts, a softening of them in love towards one another,
and this end, war as a means not only utterly fails to ac-
complish but on the contrary serves only to defeat.

From a special study of the New Testament and particularly of the significance of the Cross of Christ as bearing upon this problem of war I came to feel: first, that
where one's will in no sense enters into the committing of
an evil by another and the only means of preventing it
would be thru actions wrong in themselves, merely to
permit or allow the other to commit the evil is not to be
guilty of evil oneself; second, that for a Christian there is
no such thing as "a necessary evil" because the Cross re-

[181]

veals the fact that suffering or even an ignominious death is to be preferred to participation in evil and that the suffering or death thus incurred is in reality only the means to a larger, fuller life obtainable thru resurrection with Christ; and lastly, I came to see that the way of the Cross is the only effective way of meeting and overthrowing sin in the human heart.

I believe that the establishment of a relationship of love with God and with our fellow men is the end or purpose of life and that men's thoughts and actions in so far as they work against such a relationship are evil. When a man persists in evil, there is bound to come a time when it is no longer possible to remain indifferent to his evil actions and when it is therefore necessary to choose between either having nothing further to do with him, sometimes even going so far as to eliminate him altogether, or, out of love for him, bearing with him, suffering as a result of the disunion and of the pain which result from the sinner's actions in order that so far as oneself is concerned, union with him may never be made impossible. To choose the former of these courses is to choose the way of the sword, to choose the latter is to choose the way of forgiveness, the way of the Cross; and because of God's infinite love for men in spite of their sins, He has chosen the latter course in dealing with them and is continually bearing with men and for their sakes suffering as a result of the sins they commit in order that union with Him may never be made impossible.

As men come to realize this message of the Cross revealed to them thru others who are living and preaching it, they come to see that sin is terrible not as they had supposed because God punishes it relentlessly, but because it cuts the heart of a God who loves them with an infinite love. They come to see also that with such a God there is tremendous hope even for the worst of sinners. Thus it is, that God's very act of forgiveness revealed thru the Cross is the means whereby men's hearts are broken and they turn in repentance to be regenerated by God's spirit. They turn then from sin, not out of fear for themselves, but out of fear of wounding the heart of One who loves them and whose heart is cut by the sin they commit.

As like produces like, so God's love arouses within men a love which seeks to answer His, and in some measure, to return the love poured out for them on the Cross. Evil is driven out thru the expulsive power of a new and holy affection and finally, men strive to act towards those who sin against them, as God has acted towards them.

Having arrived at this interpretation of the Cross, which I have tried only briefly to suggest, I voluntarily returned to America in December, 1917. I was no longer able conscientiously to continue in the work of the Y.M.C.A., an organization which was playing so indispensable a part in the prosecution of the war. I was further convinced that the highest service I could render my Master and my country alike, lay either in continuing my studies in preparation for a life of definite Christian work or, if drafted, in quietly refusing to become a soldier or otherwise to serve under conscription.

On March 29th at my home in Detroit I was drafted for service in the army. Without consulting me in the matter, however, my father, to whom my present stand has been a sore trial, had my draft postponed in order to take me to Washington where he hoped by explaining my case to procure for me a bomb-proof job with the government.

Quite apart from the nature of the position which I might have been able to procure thru such a course, I felt in taking it I would be condoning conscription, which I believe is almost as great an evil as war itself, since it is not only the backbone of militarism but for many a most serious obstacle to their living the truth as they see it and to their serving God and humanity as they feel deep down in their hearts they have been called upon to serve. Accordingly, to the great disappointment of my father I was forced to turn down the Washington proposition.

On April 26th I was again drafted and this time reported at Camp Custer, Mich., where I was placed with other objectors to war; on July 1st I was examined by the board, appointed by the President, to pass on the sincerity of conscientious objectors. Altho judged sincere, owing to my refusal to accept a farm furlough or a furlough permitting me to join the Friends' Reconstruction Unit in France, I was again brought before the board at Fort Leavenworth, Kansas on July 20th, but again I refused to condone conscription by accepting the furlough offered me.

On July 26th I was transferred from Fort Leavenworth to Fort Riley, Kansas. Here I was subjected to a government policy which I hold in no small part responsible for my entering on August 19th upon a hunger strike for liberty. My action, however, was a serious mistake for it laid me open to the charge of upholding the right of

[184]

suicide and further of being false to the doctrine of non-resistance, which I hold. At the end of two weeks, therefore, I came to abandon the strike. Unfortunately I did not recognize my mistake, until I had caused the government considerable trouble. I should like, therefore, to take this opportunity of publicly acknowledging my mistake and apologizing to the government for the trouble which I caused it.

Since the hunger strike, I have sought to the best of my ability to abide by the spirit of Secretary Baker's ruling requiring conscientious objectors to cook their own food and keep themselves and their surroundings clean. But unfortunately the order given me on September 28th to assist in policing the parade grounds seemed to me so obviously to exceed the spirit of the Secretary's ruling and what I could conscientiously do, that I refused to comply with it. Since September 28th I have been confined in the guardhouse at Fort Riley.

In closing, gentlemen, I wish to state that in following the course I have and in refusing to obey the order issued me on September 28th I have been prompted by no desire to be an obstructionist or even to protest against a course of action on the part of the government which the vast majority of my countrymen heartily support. I have been prompted only by a desire to remain true to the Master whom I seek to follow. I do not believe in war or in compulsory service under any circumstances, and I cannot live as if I did. For me to accept any service under the government at the present time, I feel, would be to condone conscription and thus involve me in living a lie. Some day I may come to see that I have been wrong in taking the stand I have, but in the meantime I cannot and will not sin against the Light as I see it.

HAROLD STUDLEY GRAY

Fort Riley, Kansas
October 31, 1918

The official record of the court-martial states that when Gray had finished reading his statement, the Judge Advocate presented the following argument for the prosecution.

In the case, if the Court please, the accused went to England in 1916 as a Y.M.C.A. worker. There in England he had plenty of opportunity to see the effects of war upon the men taking part therein. Then was the time that he began to have these deep religious convictions as to the propriety of waging warfare. The fact that these deep religious or conscientious scruples did not begin to materialize until he had this opportunity to observe the effect that it had upon mankind is significant in itself. The fact that he came back to this country in 1917, that is the date I believe he said, is significant because if I remember correctly, it was about that time that England and the United States were negotiating for treaties which would allow the citizens of one country or the other to be conscripted or drafted if they were in the other country. He came back to this country and was drafted. His father took him to Washington to get what he calls a "bomb-proof job," presumably in the War Department or in some government office in Washington. Now, if the Court please, it is a matter of common knowledge, at that time there was quite some comment in the newspapers about swivel chair officers and that all men of fighting age should be taken out of their positions or out of the swivel chairs and sent to Germany. Therefore, the accused refused to accept the office job because of the possibility that he would be taken out of the swivel chair and sent to the front; in other words, his whole idea has been to evade service or any possibility of service. He speaks of the Master whom he has to follow and the love of God. True, the love of God passeth all understanding, but did the love of God keep the devil and his angels from being driven out of heaven, when he rebelled? No. The fact that He drove them out into hell shows that "the love of God" has no such meaning as the accused sets forth. Had he been in heaven would the conscientious scruples of the accused have caused him to refuse to assist in driving out the devil? Even Christ, himself, became angry with the money changers. Didn't he take a whip and drive them out of the Temple? True, he didn't kill them, but he used physical force to drive them out of his House of Prayer. I ask the Court to consider if this case is not a question of cowardice, and ask for the death penalty.

When the Judge Advocate had finished, the president of the court turned to Gray. "You, the accused, are advised that you have at this time the right to argue your case upon the facts brought out in this trial and upon the law of the case. Do you desire to argue?"

To this Gray replied, "I don't believe so, thank you." And the case was closed.

> Guardhouse, Bldg. 29
> Fort Riley, Kansas
> *November 11*

It is Monday morning and they will soon be calling for this letter which should have been written yesterday so I shall have to write fast.

Your letter of November 7th arrived yesterday afternoon. I was glad to learn that you received my letter of last week with the enclosed statement. It seems to me the celebration on Thursday about which you write was a little premature. We didn't celebrate here until this morning when the whistles in Junction City woke us all up early. I rejoice that the war is at last over. I only hope and pray that it may not mean the beginning of widespread revolution and disorder in Europe in which America will find it necessary to intervene in order to protect her investments there, but of course America could never have such a motive for intervening even if she did try to quell disorder in Europe.

I think for the present it would be best not to forward mail to me. There is a good prospect of my being in Leavenworth by next Sunday and I can then write whether it would be best to forward letters. The sixty-odd C.O.'s who still continue here will probably be shipped to Leavenworth fast now as most of them have already had their courts-martial.

Armistice Day with its joyful declaration of the cessation of war and its hope, shared by millions, that a new era of peace and goodwill had dawned, saw Harold Gray still doubtful of the decision of those who had sat in judgment at the court-martial. On the basis of the experience of Evan Thomas he believed that he would probably be given a sentence of life imprisonment at hard labor and that this sentence might thru clemency be commuted to twenty-five years. That had been the judgment passed on Thomas for his offense of defiance to the government through his refusal to eat. As to what change the signing of the Armistice with its attendant events might bring to pass, one conjecture was as good as another.

Gray's anticipation of the decision of the judges was correct. He was sentenced to life imprisonment and committed to the Disciplinary Barracks at Fort Leavenworth; upon review his sentence was commuted to twenty-five years' imprisonment at hard labor, and it was so written on the record books when on Friday, November 15, 1918, four days after the signing of the Armistice, the giant iron doors of Leavenworth swung to upon the figure of the man who for the duration of his stay was to be not Harold Studley Gray of Detroit but Prisoner Number 15175.

CHAPTER VI

I
T WAS on Armistice Day that Mr. Gray wrote to
President Wilson asking intervention in the case of his
son, Harold. No word had come to the Gray family regarding the decision of the court-martial, and the fear that
the plea of the Judge Advocate might have been granted
and the death penalty meted out haunted Mr. and Mrs.
Gray day and night. This was no easy letter to write and
ill-concealed between the thought-crowded lines is the
struggle between a father's deep affection for his oldest son
and the pained hurt that the son had done that for which
the father can find but scant sympathy in his heart.

November
eleventh
1 9 1 8.

Hon. Woodrow Wilson,
    President of the United States,
        Washington, D. C.
Dear Sir:—
    I crave the privilege of submitting for your consideration
the case of my son, Harold S. Gray, who has been held in
the guardhouse at Fort Riley, Kansas, as a conscientious
objector since September 28th and who on October 31st
was tried by court-martial at Camp Funston with the plea
by the Judge Advocate that he be given the death penalty,

and I am unable to learn as yet what sentence has been passed on him.

My son has been a most exemplary member of my household and being unusually lovable is loved and admired by all of us, though as to his views touching the evil of war and conscription under any circumstances we cannot agree with him, yet we know he is thoroly conscientious and holds his views from deep, if erroneous, religious convictions.

The Court at Camp Funston charged him with cowardice on several counts, whereas there is not a cowardly note in his nature. To hold the views he has in spite of their unpopularity at this time calls for courage of a high order. He is of such a courageous nature that the Court's threat of the death penalty in his case does not intimidate him in the least as the threat was evidently intended to do. Of all conscientious objectors his sincerity is unsurpassed, and if in his case the death penalty was recommended seriously with the full intent if possible to carry it out, it is a most terrible reflection on the character and justice of the government service somewhere.

When a young boy he joined the Central Christian Church of Detroit. In this same Christian brotherhood, tho in a different congregation, I became a member when a boy, and my father and grandfather were elders for years and died as such. My son's grandfather on his mother's side, Dr. William S. Studley, was one of the most notable members of the Methodist pulpit in the country until his death. Thus my son inherited religious tendencies. As a high school boy in his teens he was a Bible teacher both in his church and in the boys' department of the Detroit Y.M.C.A. After leaving high school he was between two and three years at Phillips Exeter Academy in New Hampshire where he led a number of the religious movements among the students and was instrumental in taking to three annual Student Conferences at Northfield the largest delegation of students ever attending that conference from Exeter Academy. When later he went to Harvard University, he continued in the same way his religious activities and influence. George Sherwood Eddy of the International Young Men's Christian Association told me that while in Harvard my son had the strongest religious influence of any student there, Mr. Eddy having had occasion in his work among the students to observe the situation very thoroly. In July, 1916 when but half thru his Harvard career, he responded to the call of the Young Men's Christian Association for secretaries abroad and sailed for England. He returned to America in December, 1917, having spent all of the time intervening in England working among English and Canadian troops and German prisoners of war. This latter work was a decidedly unpopular one so my son made few friends outside the circle of the Y.M.C.A. secretaries, and his life became rather narrowed in its vision and contact. He was twenty-two when he went to England and as it proved, was quite too young to experience all he did and keep his balance.

As I am President of the Detroit Y.M.C.A. and a member of the International Committee of the Y.M.C.A., I was able to learn from a number of sources as to the character of service my son was giving in England, and I thus learned it to be very conscientious and effective. He threw himself so completely into the work, especially in behalf of the unhappy German prisoners, was so unsparing of his physical limitations and his sympathies were so continually wrought upon in his work among suffering, unhappy prisoners that he practically broke down in June, 1917 and was induced by his "Y" associates over there to give up the work for a time and go into the country for a long needed rest. Learning of the condition he was in, his mother and I in our letters urged him not to return to work with the German prisoners when he was well enough for service again, so he did not return to that particular work, but spent most of his time in service in the American Y.M.C.A. in London, until his return to America.

His personal observations of war conditions in England and of the degrading moral effect of the war on the soldiers with whom he came in contact brought him with his deep religious nature to believe that war is wrong under all circumstances and that conscription is but surrendering one's will to the demands of the government when that will should be free to serve its higher authority, God, as the conscience dictates. A study of social conditions in England, observation of some features of capital and labor conditions there, and an acquaintance and fellowship with some influential anti-war preachers, all added to my son's deep convictions. When he left America and ever since the great war started in 1914, he was strongly anti-German and he came home from England no less anti-German— but decidedly anti-war. In the short time he was home with his family, from December, 1917 until he was obliged to report at Camp Custer, Michigan, in April following, owing to his easily upset physical condition and rather weakened nerves, I was unable to influence him to any extent to modify his views in their application to his own country. I believe I did everything that I could do reasonably and without danger of his complete physical breakdown, to get him to accord with our many Detroit friends in their loyalty to America in this war.

The boy needs a long physical and mental rest and change, for his continued internment since April, 1918 in Custer, Leavenworth, and Riley, has not helped the situation an iota. He has many qualifications for leadership, is a maker and keeper of friends, desires above all things to lead young men to clean, righteous, Christian living, has natural endowments and strong high purposes, all of which when he may be consistently released by the government, and after adequate physical rest and further college training, will make him a most valuable and effective citizen of our country.

Respectfully yours,
PHILIP H. GRAY

P.S. A letter identical with this is addressed and being sent to the Hon. Newton D. Baker, Secretary of War.

Meanwhile his arrival at Fort Leavenworth, a military prison euphemistically called "disciplinary barracks," marked the beginning of a new chapter in Gray's adventure in learning and living.

The letters for this period were briefer and somewhat less frequent than in the earlier chapters. One reason for this change was the prison regulation that allowed a prisoner a single sheet of paper a week. Some of his crowded sheets suggest a game to see how many words the pencil could squeeze into a few square inches of white paper.

A second reason was that Gray was finding himself in a situation so disheartening, forced to lead a life which by external compulsion was so unnatural and abnormal that his heart sank at finding words to speak his thoughts. And had his heart prompted his pencil to write, there was the complete assurance of the destruction which the prison censor was duty-bound to mete out to any letters which spoke the truth realistically.

No full picture of prison life at Fort Leavenworth during the winter of 1918-1919 is to be gained from these letters. For that one must turn elsewhere, and what a picture of horror it presents! The *Survey* of February 15, 1919, carries a first-hand story of the prisoners' strike, following the fire. Mr. Thomas's study, *The Conscientious Objector in America* continues the narrative for a longer period of time. Overcrowded conditions, inadequate ventilation and sanitation, outmoded methods of prison-discipline, unjust and inhumanly severe sentences made for a life and a morale wherein mind, body, and soul suffered.

But there is very little of this in Gray's letters. Indeed, there appears to be surprisingly little of it with any accompanying bitterness in his recollection of this portion of his experience.

> Fort Leavenworth, Kansas
> *November 24, 1918*

It is fortunate for the censor that my writing space is limited because there is so much I want to write about that he would never get it read if I wrote all I should like.

I have been in the D.B.'s now for over a week and frankly I am having a hard time adjusting myself to the life here. It is a real prison and "barracks" is the last word to describe the place. We reached here, twenty-two of us, from Fort Riley a week ago last Friday. After a thoro searching we were quartered for the first night in the sub-basement opposite the cells containing most of my friends who have refused to work. The treatment they are receiving is most severe. I came here fully intending to work, but I hadn't been here long before I was all upset and didn't know what to do. Conditions were not at all as I expected. Everything is under the military and seems to contribute to the military. Last Sunday when called before the executive, I told him I didn't see how I could do anything under the military or for them, and that I therefore could accept no work. Thirteen of the twenty-two took a similar stand. But I was soon up in the air again. The whole thing seemed so near a fifty-fifty proposition with pride and desire to be with my old friends pulling so strongly on the side of solitary bread and water and handcuffs, that I finally gave up trying to reason my way out and just threw myself completely on God for guidance.

[196]

The result was that for better or for worse I decided on Monday to give the work a trial at least.

On Tuesday I was put in the fourth gang and set at shoveling cinders all day. At night I was completely all in. I have shoveled cinders every day since. The stiffness and soreness of the first few days are largely gone, but frankly my heart is not much in my work. In addition to shoveling cinders our detail helps unload freight cars and carry cordwood into the bakery. It is all pretty heavy work but fortunately for the most part out-of-doors. I am learning the meaning of "hard labor" five hours in the morning and four in the afternoon. I understand there is a clerical vacancy in the hospital which there is some prospect of my being assigned to in the course of this week, but nothing is certain. Already I have turned down two jobs because they were too military in nature, one a carpentering job on the signal corps buildings and another pressing soldiers' uniforms. The hospital work or any farming is work I feel I can conscientiously do, but should I be ordered to perform work which is military in character, I should refuse at once and take the consequences. As I think I wrote you, I believe there is a big difference between working under conscription and working under compulsion. When a man serves under conscription, it means either that he believes he can serve God and humanity best in one of the branches of service open to him under the draft, or that he is willing to let the state dictate how he shall use his life, but when a man serves under compulsion he need only believe that the work he does is not wrong in itself. The very fact that he has to be imprisoned and compelled is proof that he believes God has some work for him to do other than any of those opportunities open to him under the draft and that he believes God and not the state has the right to say how he shall use his life.

I shall not write what I think of the place both because of the censor and the brief space allowed me. It seems indeed strange that those of us who advocate a better way of dealing with evil and evildoers should have such a splendid opportunity to study the old system by being victims of it. If it is true that God is in any sense essential to the redemption of an evildoer, a prison like this is the worst place in the world to send him. From five in the morning on we are constantly on the move with no time to think, much less to pray. At night I have been so tired that I have read a chapter in my Bible over and over without knowing what I was reading.

My ears fairly ring with profanity and I would give most anything to be alone where it is quiet once in a while. Fortunately my cellmate, a Mennonite, is a very quiet, pleasant fellow, but we have almost nothing in common. Unless I am able to adjust myself better to the life here in the course of the next few weeks, it will indeed be a cross if I have to live out the twenty-five years which I have been sentenced for. When Jesus cried out on the cross, "My God, my God, why hast thou forsaken me?" I wonder if it could have been a condemnation of a system of dealing with criminals which made it difficult for even Christ to feel in close contact with God. And yet from whence comes the power to conquer sin and evil in our own lives except as we are in contact with him? Not thru

[198]

war and prisons but thru the Cross of Christ, and the world will never be redeemed until men put their trust completely in the latter by abandoning forever the former. It is the world's only hope. May God hasten the day!

Your loving and devoted son,

15175

December 1

I am writing in the office of the hospital where I was assigned to duty last Tuesday. The position came as a great relief in many respects. The work, what there is of it, is mostly typewriting, which is just the sort of work I wanted. The men here are very nice and belong to the medical corps, not to the prison guard; this makes a great difference in the treatment you receive. Altho there is not a great deal of work to do, the main attraction here is the meals which tho no better than those at Custer are in marked contrast to the general mess where I ate the first week and a half I was here. Fortunately my assignment came just before Thanksgiving so I was able to enjoy a real Thanksgiving dinner. Altho I enjoyed it very much, I couldn't help thinking of the dinner that I knew you folks were having at home. Needless to say I would have given a good deal to have been there.

Letters mean a good deal to a man here. They help to break the monotony of the life. Last Monday I drew Emerson's *Essays, Second Series,* from the library and have nearly finished them. But at best what an existence this is! I have a bad cold and my physical condition reminds me of my mental, or vice versa; I feel stifled. What a wonder-

[199]

ful thing liberty is, the right and opportunity to get away from people once in a while, to be able to breathe deep. I go to the movies, which they have here on Sundays, in an attempt just to lose myself, but the pictures are so poor and the comments which one hears from the men on every side often so vulgar as to make it a relief to have it over, and yet I persist in going next time if it is only to break the monotony. I presume my cold is very largely responsible for my present state of mind, yet this does not account for all of it.

I remember May telling me how many of the miners at Denby Main enlisted out of sheer craving for a change from the monotonous life which they live. I appreciate now the force of her remark. Anything to escape from such slavery and how real economic slavery is too! It is salvation, not safety, this old world needs, and salvation comes only thru Christ for he alone can conquer selfishness, which is the root of all the trouble. We see the hands of thieves and murderers and they are red. We picture that our own hands are clean, but it is only because they are bound so tightly behind our backs by sin that we cannot see them. When the Master comes and loosens them and we behold, they are red too and it hurts us very much to look at them. The old order has got to go but it will never go thru so-called socialism or violence; it must go because men's hearts have been changed by the redemptive power of the Cross. And that means crosses for us too. It means trusting absolutely to Christ and taking the consequences, and trusting Christ means doing nothing but the right.

When we trust in a wrong to make things right, we are putting our trust in the devil and not in Christ.

December 9

When I was first detailed for work in the hospital nearly two weeks ago, I was placed in the office where I helped make out records, but since then I have been shifted to a ward and now have a regular position as an orderly. At first I did not like it much, but now I think I have the best job in the prison. There is not a great deal of work to do and when I have helped clean up the ward in the morning, it is mainly a case of waiting on patients so that I have quite a bit of time to read. I am in the guards' ward, and there is a ward-master and another prisoner acting as nurse besides myself. Both of these men are very nice especially 13386, who is an old Detroit boy. He coaches me on the nursing and what with the manual and all I hope to pick up a good bit on the subject before the winter is over.

Last Monday I drew some of Henry Drummond's addresses from the library, and I confess I have seldom read anything so fine or inspiring. Unfortunately there are no other of his books in the library so that I shall have at least one thing to look forward to when I get out of here. I am reading now some of Phillips Brooks's addresses. They are very good but hardly equal to Drummond's.

More and more the tremendous need of men for Christ is burning itself in upon me. If I ever had any faith in a government resting on force, my experience here has shattered the last lingering remnants of that faith. The trouble with the world is selfishness and the only thing the legislatures, law courts, and prisons can do is alter the form perhaps, but they can never touch the trouble. Indeed it is my firm belief that they only accentuate it. What a tremendous need there is here among the men for just the sort of thing which Christ alone can give them, a new life. Once I get my stride I think I am going to be very, very happy here in the opportunity for Christian service which has been given me.

I want a good college textbook in geology. I think perhaps I can get permission to have it sent in if they do not have it here. If I ever get out of here, I want to take a thoro course in agriculture with a view some day to working out my communistic ideas of reconstruction. The bolsheviks may have the right ideals, but they sure have the wrong method, or perhaps I should say far-from-the-best-method of attaining those ideals. Altho there are undoubtedly many noble souls in the socialist movement, I am afraid it is at bottom prompted by selfishness.

I am very sorry the government has seen fit to take the attitude which it has towards the C.O.'s here. The very sort of injustice and tyranny which the socialists make such capital of in their attacks is ripening here and must inevitably become known some day, I fear, not to the honor and credit of the U. S. You have mentioned in your letters that you are not inactive on my behalf. You won't let your activity run along channels which might arouse hatred, anger, or bitterness towards the government? I would rather serve my whole sentence than be released because a certain kind of pressure had been brought to bear upon the government. Thanks for your last letter of December 1st. May Christ be with you.

December 16

I am not a betting man but if I were I think I would be willing to stake a good deal on the assertion that I am the happiest man in this prison, and I haven't received a notice of immediate release or any little thing like that either. The source of my happiness is my work. It may not sound very big to say that I am just a hospital orderly, but as I am concerned with realities not with appearances, I don't care how it sounds. The truth is I have a job that is bigger than I am and one which affords a wonderful opportunity for service. Altho I am on duty practically twelve hours a day, from six in the morning to six at night, seven days of the week, the time fairly flies. I can hardly wait to get over to the ward in the morning to start the day.

Last week for two or three days I was special nurse for a bad case of pneumonia. The man was delirious a good deal of the time, but took quite a fancy to me so that he preferred to have me wait on him to anyone else. Towards the end he got pretty restless, and so remembering some of my own days in bed I volunteered to read to him. It seemed to quiet him a lot, even tho I doubt if he understood any of the story I read to him. Even Thursday, the day he died, he asked me to read to him again. That night I watched the doctors draw a gallon of pus from his right lung. They thought after that he would pull thru till the next day. I wasn't very keen about changing places with the night nurse when the time came but I had to. He died very suddenly a couple of hours after I left. The old guard was carried away today to be shipped to relatives in S. D.

Now I am just running around waiting on general patients in the ward. I get an opportunity every now and then to talk a bit and the conversation not infrequently concerns itself with serious things. They are an interesting bunch of men, these guards, with lots of real stuff in them. What unrealized possibilities we are constantly discovering in men! When men begin to think in terms of individuals, I believe the world will go forward very fast. The modern world has forgotten that there is such a thing as an individual. Men are just cogs in a machine, "hands" that is all. What a crime it is to think of men that way instead of to realize the divine that's in them! Men here talk a good deal about when they are going to get released and all sorts of wild rumors float about, but frankly I am not very much interested. God has given me a man's job and I am not keen to quit until He is ready to put me at something else. I get quite a bit of time to read thru the day. I am studying nursing a good bit but I still have time to read a magazine now and then. Speaking of magazines, I wonder if you would mind getting the *Nation* for a year so that when I get home I can see some of the back numbers.

I have just drawn Emerson's *Essays, First Series,* from the library to read evenings. I am going to put in a request to get some of the books out of my valise, especially *Concerning Prayer* by Streeter and others. It has such wonderful stuff in it. We are locked in our cells almost immediately after supper so that we have the evening until nine to read. At that time the lights go out. I have been sleeping fine; my cold and cough are practically all gone and I am feeling fine. To be sure I am not getting quite as much outdoor air and exercise as I should like, but the ward is well ventilated and there is enough work to keep certain muscles at least fairly active. The eats at the hospital are fine. You must join your prayers with mine that I may render our Master very real service while I am here. How I love you all!

The letter of December 23rd, largely descriptive of the prison and prison life, is addressed to his younger sister.

December 23

It is now over five weeks since I first came to the D.B.'s, and if you know as little about this place as I did before I came here, perhaps you would enjoy a bit of a description, for this is a very different world from any I have ever lived in before.

Altho I understand a very considerable tract of land is attached to the prison for the growing of crops, raising of cattle, etc., the prison grounds proper are about the size of the Waterworks Park, Detroit, or perhaps a little smaller; they are surrounded by a broad, high wall with watch towers at short intervals along the wall in which armed sentries are constantly stationed. Within this enclosure are several buildings, the hospital, power plant, workshops, executive buildings, all of which are more or less overpowered by the enormous prison itself. The prison, or barracks, as they call it, is built in the form of a large rotunda off of which radiate eight wings, four of which contain the cells, the large middle one the auditorium, mess hall, shower room and barber shop, clothing supply room, etc., and the three smaller wings shops and offices of one sort or another. The cell wings are roughly about one hundred fifty feet long by forty or fifty feet wide and high enough to contain eight tiers of cells. Two of these tiers are in the basement and sub-basement but six tiers rise one above another in one gigantic room; with the ranges or galleries running around each tier, they remind one very much of the side of a great ocean liner. Each cell is about nine by five and a half feet and in the fourth wing, where I was first quartered, each cell contains a bowl and washbasin with running water. The reason for this is that in this wing the prisoners are always locked in their cells when in the wing. In addition to the bowl and basin each cell contains a double-decked bed so that two men can be accommodated in each cell.

Before I became a hospital orderly a day passed about as follows: Shortly before 5 A.M. the lights in all the cells are turned on and soon afterwards a room-orderly awakens all who eat early mess. These include men on special duty who must be at their work before the regular hours, together with all who have not been in the prison over a month, for during the first month of a man's imprisonment here he is required to take early morning drill and must therefore eat at the early or six o'clock mess. Immediately on being awakened we rise, wash, and dress in the prison uniform, conspicuous because each piece is marked with the prisoner's number in figures measuring two or two and one-half inches high placed on the back of the coat and shirt and on the front of each trouser leg just above the knee where it can be readily seen. We are known and addressed only by our numbers. My number is 15175. There are three classes of prisoners. The first class, which contains practically all of the men, wear white numbers; the second class, red; and the third, yellow. All the men in solitary are in yellow numbers.

As soon as we have dressed we fold up our blankets and arrange all our belongings not on our backs in order upon the bed. These are not many and consist of a hand towel, soap, toothbrush and powder, brush and comb, a suit of overalls if we do not have them on and a raincoat, overcoat and cap. These with our Bible and one library book are all we are allowed to have. With the exception of our Bibles everything is issued to us, and we are allowed to bring nothing in from the outside when we come. Our clothes have no pockets in them with the exception of one rear pocket in our trousers in which to carry a blue bandana handkerchief. The overcoats are interesting because tho now dyed black they were once blue and were worn by the soldiers in the Civil War.

After sweeping out our cells and dusting and polishing thoroly, we line up for early mess; that comes at six o'clock followed immediately by two other messes which are necessary in order to feed the thirty-four hundred-odd prisoners, as not more than fifteen hundred can be fed at one time. The mess hall is a huge room with rows of seats running crossways, with one aisle down the center of the hall and two aisles on either side. The men all face one way and the rows of seats resemble a schoolroom with desks. The plates are all passed towards the aisles to be filled. Here the K.P.'s walk back and forth with large boilers of food.

Breakfast over we have half an hour of drill out in the yard. Owing to my drill work at Exeter I caught on to it here pretty quickly, and the last two weeks of it I led the class of over a hundred men. After drill we line up in a column of fours and are dispatched by gangs to our work. The first week or so I was on a gang, the fourth, which shoveled cinders at the power plant. At twelve o'clock was dinner and at one o'clock we were back at our work for a four-hour stretch. After supper in the evening we went immediately to our cells and were locked in. At eight and later at eight-forty-five we stood at our cell-door with our arms folded while we were counted. At nine o'clock the lights go out and we are supposed to be in bed. Once a week in the evening we can draw one library book for the week; twice a week we get a shave in the barber shop, once a week we get a shower bath and clean underwear and socks, and once a week we draw writing paper and smoking tobacco or chewing gum. We are allowed no money and indeed it would be of little use to us here as there is nothing to buy. Every Sunday evening we have a movie show and sometimes also on Tuesday evenings but not always.

At present my daily routine differs slightly from that outlined above. In the first place, I am no longer in a locked cell, but in the seventh or honor wing where the cells are all open, and tho the wing is always locked, we are free to visit other cells and chat with our friends in the wing. Also, I am on duty twelve instead of nine hours, and every day instead of getting my Saturday afternoon and Sundays off. Moreover I now eat at the hospital instead of at the barracks. At first I did not like to change to the seventh wing, but there are some splendid fellows there, C.O.'s who have been here some time, and I am very happy to be with them. They are mostly political objectors. An old cellmate of mine is now next door to me. My cellmate is a sort of I.W.W., very interesting, who deserted because he hated the army so. When he was caught after nine months, he was given twenty years.

The longer I am here the more I realize what a pitiful failure a prison is as an institution to make people better. Until I came here I never believed men capable of such rottenness, yet I cannot but feel that the trouble is by no means all with the men themselves but with the very spirit and atmosphere existing here, which the institution itself helps to produce. Men grow towards God and away from selfishness and sensuality by association with those who are nobler, purer, and better than themselves, those whose very presence awakens new and higher hopes and aspirations; yet it is from just such people that prison cuts men off. Here they associate with men no better and often worse than themselves with the result that far from being regenerated they are dragged still lower. It is just such an institution as this which convinces me that the traditional conception of hell as a place where evildoers go after death was invented by men and does not exist in reality. God couldn't be so stupid! As for men's suffering the result of their sins, they do that right here on this earth. One need only live with those whose selfishness has separated them from God and from the deepest in their fellow men to realize how keenly they suffer the result of their sins, even tho they are often for the most part quite unconscious of their suffering because they have never known the real joy of living.

When Jesus came to redeem men from selfishness, I see now why he was constantly being accused of associating with the publicans and sinners. That is the only way to redeem them, not by isolating them or turning from them. As in the case of Jesus, his way may mean kicking one's reputation to the winds. It was not the way the respectables who moved in polite society took, but Jesus saw that it was the way of God and that was all that mattered.

Tomorrow will be Christmas Eve. How I should love to be at home with you all at this time but it is not God's will and God always has a good reason. I am very well and very happy. I love my work and I am making some wonderful friends. My love and the season's greetings to you all.

January 1

I have just had dinner and everything in the ward being shipshape, I have seated myself in an invalid's chair by the side of our worst patient at present, who is practically paralyzed and helpless with rheumatism. If this letter, therefore, seems disconnected, it will be because I have had to get up every few minutes while writing it to wait on some one.

I am more and more convinced that this prison experience was the greatest thing that could have happened to me. God's hand is certainly in it somewhere. As a mission field it is the greatest imaginable. If I should actually have to serve my full sentence here, I could never, never say I did not have a chance in life, for wherever there are men who are living lives apart from God we have our chance; geography isn't the determining factor. With things as they are just at present, today is so full of opportunity for unselfish service and a chance to show forth the Christian spirit that I have no time to consider tomorrow. The time is going very fast and I suppose the reason is that I am so happy. Believe me, prison bars or poverty aren't the things that determine our happiness. As I look back over the past year, I think the last half of it has been the happiest I have ever spent. How often those lines in *The Passing of the Third Floor Back* come to my mind: "It isn't poverty but the fear of poverty that drives out love," and how easily "prison bars" might be substituted for "poverty."

Christmas passed here much like any other day except that we had a very fine turkey dinner, indeed one of the best dinners I ever ate, and the two other meals were good too. In the evening we had a good movie. I am finding considerable time for reading. I find it is possible to have books sent in and so I shall want either you or Mother to send me a book each week. At present I am reading H. G. Wells's new book on education, *Joan and Peter*, and next I am going to tackle Romain Rolland's *Jean Christophe.*

I have recently learned that our writing privileges have

been extended to two sheets a week instead of one, provided we can get the paper. As my cellmate never writes, he gives his paper to me, so beginning next week I hope to write two letters a week instead of one, tho both will come home in the same envelope.

Give my love and very best wishes for the New Year to all the family.

January 14

Now in addition to doing the cleaning and waiting on the patients, I have the diets and most of the medications to look after. I don't mind the additional responsibility but it gives me less time to myself than formerly. Last Sunday when the major made the first inspection since the beginning of the year, he said our ward was by far the neatest and cleanest. I am not altogether surprised for I spent nearly twenty-four hours scrubbing the floor on my hands and knees during afternoons when I was not otherwise engaged. I don't think such a thing had ever been done before in the history of the hospital. It is so much easier doing one's work when one can take a little pride in doing it.

A week ago Saturday Judge Mack and the board visited the prison and interviewed the C.O.'s. My turn came about twelve P.M. that night after a long hard day in the hospital. I was so tired I could hardly hold my head up. I turned down the farm furlough as before, for the same reasons as before, and was just leaving the room when one of the majors who interviewed me at the hospital at Fort

Riley and who is now stationed here called me over and asked me what I was doing here. I told him and said I was quite in love with my work. Judge Mack overheard me and asked me to explain why I could do hospital work here and not outside. I tried to explain the distinction which is so clear in my own mind between working under conscription and working under compulsion and seemed to make a bad mess of my explanation.

I have come in contact with a most interesting group of radicals here. . . . Every Sunday evening we have a symposium at which we discuss various problems of interest to radicals. I am the only "believer" in the group but the others seem to be interested in what I have to say. A week ago Sunday the topic was "The Fullness of Life" and I spoke from a believer's point of view. Last Sunday the discussion was on "The Social Obligation to Marry." There are several upholders of a sort of free love in the group. While I disagree, of course, with many views put forward at these symposiums, they certainly furnish food for thought. I am meeting men who conscientiously hold views which I never dreamed men could hold honestly and sincerely, and it is a great thing for me. "As evil is yet wider than we dream, so good is deeper." It seems as if as fast as I have my eyes opened to the evil in men's hearts, God opens my eyes to the good which is there too, patiently waiting for the coming of love to make it blossom forth. I am often amazed even among the so-called religious C.O.'s how little faith they have in God and the power of love as the only way! How different it is to have faith in God compared with merely believing that there is a God!

A prison can be a great place to stimulate thought processes; at least, I seem to be doing a deal of thinking here and I fear it is not to the advantage of the present social order. In the searching light of Christ, conscription is not the only social institution which I find it impossible to justify. Even if I am released from here without serving my full sentence, I may yet live to serve many years behind bars. The man who seeks to live true to his deepest convictions may not always have an easy road to travel, but it certainly is a worth-while one if for no other reason than the inward satisfaction which it brings. Before we can free others from a share in the sins of society, we must first free ourselves. And who has not tried without becoming wonderfully sympathetic with others and especially the outcasts of society?

I am as well as can be expected under the circumstance. The wings are kept so warm at night that it is almost impossible to sleep with any covers on, and even then I often lie awake and wage war on my bedfellows when I should much prefer to be asleep. If God made bedbugs, I wonder why He had to make so many? My, what a blessing it will be if I ever get free to be able to sleep in a cool, ventilated room, get a cold bath and shave myself in the morning, wear B.V.D.'s and get out where I can exercise. But I am not complaining. These are never privileges of prison life and I prefer spiritual freedom with physical bondage to physical freedom with even a wee bit of spiritual bondage. With all its hardships life is a glorious thing.

January 28

It must seem strange for a man in prison to give as his excuse for not writing that he has been very busy, yet such is in a large measure at least the explanation for not writing last week. To be sure I was rather tired all week and found it necessary to prod myself with my will to get things done, and therefore, I did no more than I had to. Also I found H. G. Wells's *Joan and Peter* most absorbing, as well as Carpenter's *Love's Coming of Age*. Altho there is little of any importance to write, at least that I think best to record in a letter, still I know that if my letters are looked forward to at home as much as I look forward to receiving yours here, they are much missed when not received on time. My apology for disappointing you last week.

The discharge of one hundred thirteen C.O.'s here has caused considerable comment, not all by any means favorable. I am surprised that practically all of them signed the pay roll. I would serve my time before I would sign it. If you folks are doing anything to facilitate my release, I wish you would direct your efforts to the release of all the military prisoners for there are many soldiers here who are the victims of as great injustice as any of the C.O.'s. If you want to check the spread of discontent and bolshevism, get busy on this prison proposition. Full prisons are a stock weapon in the hands of revolutionists, especially when the prisoners are the victims of gross injustice and ought never to have seen the inside of a place like this.

For some weeks past I have been acting as nurse and orderly here in the guards' ward often with as many as twenty-one patients to attend to with all sorts of things wrong with them, even three cases of mumps. It has been exceedingly profitable and interesting even if occasionally pretty tiring work. But I see by the hospital bulletin board tonight that next month I am to be a full-fledged nurse in the surgical ward. One of two. My doctor must have given me a good recommend. It will be much more complicated work, I presume, but for that reason probably more interesting and instructive. If I am absolutely up against it when I get out of here, perhaps I could get a job in a hospital. Altho the problem of what to do when I get out is not a very immediate or pressing one, still it is causing me considerable thought.

In the interval between letters there had occurred at Leavenworth the prisoners' strike, staged as a protest-gesture against overcrowding, poor food, and general mismanagement. No reference, however, could be made in the letters to this or to any of the matters so important in the minds of the prisoners for fear of the censor.

February 18

In spite of the fact that in both your letters of January 29th and that of February 8th, you refer to my release as if it were an assured fact, I still find myself here under the necessity of writing. Indeed unless your assurance is based on something more substantial than the facts which I possess, I fear I am destined to write to you for some time to come. I never did care much for letter writing and I care less for it now when I have to be so careful lest the censor take offense at something I say.

Last week Monday as a result mostly of hard work and insufficient sleep I came down with a genuine old attack of grippe with a fairly high temperature and pretty severe pains in my back and legs. Saturday evening for the first time during the week my temperature dropped to normal and Sunday I was discharged from the hospital for duty. I was pretty weak but still able to get about.

I wonder if you who have access to privacy appreciate what a privilege you have. Most men think of freedom in terms of material self-indulgence. I think of it in terms of getting where I can be all, all alone for at least a few hours every day. Men as well as flowers and plants are unable to grow in overcrowded conditions. I know that I am not growing. I see now why slums produce the people they do. Why, we wouldn't think of breeding live stock under conditions similar to those which exist in some of our American slums.

At present I am reading the first volume of Romain Rolland's *Jean Christophe*, which is perhaps the greatest book which has been produced in my times. Rolland's style is perfectly wonderful. I began reading the book out loud to a fellow while he was in my ward at the hospital with a pair of bad eyes. I used to sit down by his bedside whenever I got a few spare moments. He seemed to enjoy my reading and we have continued reading it together even here in the wing. Just as soon as I get thru writing this, I shall go down to his cell and read some more.

I am no longer working in the guards' ward at the hospital but in the surgical ward. The work is much more interesting and brings me in contact with a wider variety of cases. Just at present I am more or less special nurse for a case of empyema. The man is not expected to live long as one lung is entirely gone and the poison is slowly eating into the other. It is rather disagreeable work especially dressing the wound on account of the smell. But some one has to do it and why shouldn't I?

The need of more air and exercise may force me to leave the hospital in the course of the next month or so. I am waiting just now to see if anything promises to develop in the near future along the line of release. Personally I see little hope.

March 2

For some reason mail has been slow in coming and I have missed it very much. When occasionally a man's spirits fall below normal, there is nothing like a few letters from home and friends to put things right again.

Last week we finished the first volume of *Jean Christophe*, six hundred pages. It is perfectly wonderful. By chance also I procured Drummond's *Natural Law in the Spiritual World* and read that too last week. It was great and helped to clarify a lot of things.

I am still working at the hospital and I shan't leave

until my patient, 14077, either recovers or "Goes West." Because his case is so disagreeable to handle, he has been horribly neglected in the past, and now that he is getting at least a little better care and attention, he has become attached to my services. I don't feel like deserting him and the end may not be far off. I am really feeling tolerably fit now. Thanks for all your fine, birthday wishes. The day passed uneventfully. How dear you all are to me!

March 26

This is no letter, only a line to let you know I am well and happy. I did not dare to let another day go by without writing for fear you might worry. It is after eight o'clock and I am now waiting for the O.D. count and then lights go out. Fred[1] and I just got in from a lovely walk about the post. I had no trouble whatever in getting a barracks parole one day last week, and Monday I was put on the eight o'clock daily check list so that I can go out after six when I am off duty at the hospital.

I am working pretty hard these days but oh, what interesting work it is! I am a real surgical assistant, helping with all major operations and personally dressing practically all of the surgical cases. The day after you were here, I assisted at my first operation when I held a leg while a wonderful surgeon amputated it.

I hardly think I ever learned so much in so short a time as I have the last two weeks since you were here.

---

[1] Gray's cellmate who was serving as editor of the prison paper, *Stray Shots.*

At times I have gotten dreadfully tired but I guess that is all part of the game. I don't think anything ever fascinated me more than this work. It is by all odds the best job in the hospital.

Sunday Fred and I took a nice walk. It was my first outside the wall. It made me almost regret having taken a parole because I felt for the first time the real character of the place I am in and the life I have been living. I feel no bitterness.

April 1

Father dear, the months since we were last together have wrought some changes in me. I think we are going to understand each other better when next we meet. In prison one frequently gets to thinking over the past and scenes which I thought I had forgotten come back every now and then with striking vividness. How invariably you play a part in these reminiscences! Even now for some unknown reason a lump comes into my throat as I think of our first visit to Mackinac. There were just the two of us and we had such fun, didn't we? Do you remember my trying to vault a stream and having the pole stick in the middle of it so that I got all wet trying to get across, and then the lemonade at that Stag Inn or whatever it was called? Some day, perhaps, I shall be out of here and in need of a change. I wonder if you and I might not get away again together on some trip as we used to do when I was more of a boy than I am now.

My parole pass is doing me a world of good. I can get

out now every evening and every Sunday afternoon. The country around here is beautiful with many delightful walks. There is one especially which runs along the top of a ridge of hills from which one obtains the most delightful views. At first I did not like my parole because it made me feel so acutely the prison life I am forced to live, but that is all gone now. My mind has cleared a lot and I never felt better.

I am not so optimistic about my early release as I once was. I fear we are in for quite a siege of it still.

Later (evening)

I just got in from a lovely walk after putting Fred in the hospital with a temperature of 103. He has never really been well since he had the pneumonia and prison is no place to recuperate in. I wish he was out of here. Thank goodness, I have not had to eat at the prison mess these past four months; otherwise I don't know whether I could have stood it physically. Much of Fred's trouble, I think, is with his stomach.

When informed by telegram of his grandmother's death, Gray wrote:

April 13

There are times when prison is an annoying encroachment on a man's liberty and I have just experienced one of these times. Since, however, I cannot come in person and convey to you and Father and the others the deep, deep sympathy which I feel, I must needs send it by letter. My prayers are with you all.

Apropos of a friend's comment paying respect to the position of the sincere C.O. Gray wrote in his weekly letter:

April 13, cont.

Apparently one woman with a son in France (or is it Germany, now?) is not in the least bitter towards those of us who could not see things quite as others did. I hope my actions in taking the stand I have are never misunderstood as a condemnation of the actions of others, but only as an honest effort to live true to the light as I see it.

Since my last letter I have been moved to new quarters out of a cell and even out of the great prison barracks. Last week all of the paroles were transferred into an old but very roomy and comfortable barracks. There are no bars on the windows and we all sleep in big barracks rooms along the walls, much the same as at Custer only not so crowded. I am right by a window which I open at night so as to enjoy plenty of fresh air. It is not at all like being in prison with no sentry to stop you as you go in and out of the building. It is almost across the street from the hospital, so very handy.

April 15

I am all wrapped up in my work at the hospital and beginning very seriously to wonder whether surgery may not be my calling in life. Certainly I have never found anything which fascinated me more or for which in many respects I seemed better qualified. The use of instruments seems to come natural to me. Few fields offer a better opportunity for service. It means hard work and steady plodding but I seem to be pretty good at that sort of thing. Furthermore it might prove a better angle to come at my community idea than farming. Already I have begun to dream dreams and see visions. It would indeed be strange if I should discover my place in the sun in prison but God moves in a mysterious way!

After some little trouble about my parole I have finally succeeded in being placed on the eight o'clock check list for recreation only, being probably the only man here granted that privilege of going out daily between six and eight in the evening for a walk. I have been out regularly the last week and as a result am in tiptop physical condition.

Last night I heard unofficially that my clemency slip had come back from Washington with twenty-two years cut, leaving me three altogether. Apparently there is no rhyme nor reason to these cuts because ——, who took the same identical stand as I did and was with me at Fort Riley receiving the same sentence, got an immediate release a few days ago, and —— and a fellow named ——, both in my class, got eighteen months each. Fred's clemency has not yet come back from Washington but I look for his to be an "immediate." As Fred says, the ways of the War Department are inscrutable. I hate to think of missing another one or two years of college altho I know that God must have some good reason for keeping me here. I think I shall word that last sentence differently; I do not think it is God's will at all that I should be here but being kept here as a result of others' sins, I believe He will give me as great an opportunity to testify for Him here as He would give me on the outside and that is the sole thing that matters. So long as I refuse to compromise with evil, I can leave the rest to God.

Mr. Morrison wrote me a wonderful letter after his visit and a day or so ago his little book, *The Family Altar*, arrived together with the box of stationery Father sent. I began to read it Sunday, being the first day of the week. I ought to finish it one month from the day I shall be eligible for home parole. In the front of the book Mr. Morrison has written something like this, as I recall, "To Harold S. Gray, in bonds but more free than the free."

My noon hour is up and there is work to be done so I shall not begin another sheet. Love to all.

May 7

It has been a long time since I last wrote, and tho Father's visit in a sense took the place of a letter, it is now over two weeks since he was here.

Father's visit was considerable of a surprise as he probably told you because for some reason or other I had the idea that he would come on a Saturday and stay over Sunday. Believe me, it was great when I was called up to the captain's office and found Father and Philip [Gray's younger brother] awaiting me. I was especially glad to find Philip there, both because I wanted to see him and have him see the D.B. and also because it afforded him and Father an opportunity of taking a trip together. I know what those trips used to mean to me and I rejoice that my brother is not to be deprived of them. I was sorry not to be able to spend more time with them but as it was, we probably visited under about as ideal conditions as are possible here even if the time was short. The walk we took is the prettiest I know of in these parts and afforded them the best bird's-eye view of the prison and post generally. Father's visit meant a great deal to me in several ways among which was the assurance that there is to be no strained relationship between us as a result of my present stand.

The time has gone rapidly since we were together and several changes have taken place, all, I feel, for the better. As the work of the dressing room increased with the addition of several new empyemas as well as a more complicated and thoro method of treating them after the operation, I found myself greatly pressed for time and realized that some sort of readjustment was necessary. The surgeon had furthermore practically cleared up all the pus operations and was about to begin on clean cases the week Father was here, and as he planned to keep the clean cases and the pus cases absolutely separate with separate wards and everything, I realized that I was out of luck, so to speak, when it came to the operations unless I was to drop the pus work altogether.

On the Monday following Father's visit I was given the choice of doing all the pus dressings or having absolutely nothing to do with them and devoting my entire time to the clean operating room. As the position as the only male operating room nurse is to my mind the most desirable one in the hospital, barring none, I was not at all sure that as a prisoner I would stand a chance of getting it, but the gods were with me for I seem to have landed the job at the request of the surgeon, who I learned later had made the remark that he had watched me several times without my being aware of it while I was engaged in doing dressings and was much pleased with my work. I am now in the operating room with no other duties. So far we have only had one appendicitis and two hernia operations, at both of which I had a splendid opportunity to view what was going on. There is not going to be a great deal of operating so that my job promises to give me much more spare time to myself than previously; that will be a godsend. For example, both yesterday and today we had no operations and my time has been spent scrubbing the walls a little and making myself a pair of slippers out of an old blanket. Soon I hope to begin on some of the many, many letters I owe my friends. My long silence is beginning to bother me. I wonder what my friends think of me for not writing.

Last week Fred and I were moved over to the C.O. barracks in the stockade back of the prison. The change is much for the best. The barracks itself is very similar to our barracks at Custer, which you remember. The air is much fresher, and there is a delightful view facing the ridge along which Father and Philip and I took our walk. Everything is fairly new and clean with *no* bedbugs. . . . Yet what a failure I have made of things in comparison with what I might have done had I not permitted my prayer life to get shot to pieces! The hospital has crowded into first place, I fear. It is the old, old story of things perfectly good and admirable in themselves stepping in between us and God. Unless I can reverse things and re-adjust my life with God in first place, I shall have to pull out of the hospital, much as I love the work.

I have received two letters from you and two from Father since the latter's visit. Sometimes I wonder if you do not suffer much more as a result of the few discomforts which I am forced to put up with than I do. It is amazing what it is possible to get used to, and I have gotten used to a great deal which I never think of any more. Truly I am very comfortable. The only quarrel I have at present is with myself, not my surroundings. I am ashamed to realize that my life is not so deep and close to God as it might be and as I want to have it. Will you pray for me that I may gain a deeper, richer prayer life?

Sunday will be Mothers' Day. How very, very much I owe to my mother! At times it has seemed as if you alone understood me and what I was driving at. My stand must often have been so difficult to comprehend and sympathize with! I wonder how many mothers could have been as big and noble about it as you have been? Not many, of that I am sure. Truly I have God to be thanked for the dearest and most wonderful mother in the world. May He make me worthy of her!

May 28

Since writing you Fred has received word thru Roger

[227]

Baldwin that the Friends are considering sending units to Germany. . . . As a matter of fact the idea of going to Germany with the Friends to try and heal some of the bitterness which the war has produced is one which appeals very strongly indeed to me, but I guess the university is my place for a few years more anyway.

Mother dear, there certainly are times when I would give a great deal to talk to you face to face rather than have to write, for sometimes it is so hard for me to explain things and now is one of those times. In a few days I may be placed in solitary confinement. Partly because of my desire to spare you any unnecessary anxiety and partly because I really felt I would eventually decide things in a way which would not cause trouble, I have not written or said anything to you about my dislike of folding my arms to officers. When I decided to work, I rather took the view that the folding of arms was only a prison regulation to assure an officer that a man did not carry concealed weapons. But while this may have been the origin of the practice, I have come more and more to feel that it is an act of worship which I can no longer tolerate. As Fred puts it, we are willing to work but not to worship, and the folding of arms, which is nothing more nor less than a salute, is an act of worship which both of us have come strongly to feel is inconsistent with all we stand for. Accordingly several weeks ago, both of us gave up the practice. Wherever possible we have deliberately avoided officers and where this has been impossible, we have had the good fortune not to have the matter noticed, thanks perhaps to the lax discipline here of late.

CHARACTER "BAD"

At cantonment six where the C.O.'s are quartered, practically everyone either deliberately refused or failed to fold his arms at count and the matter was overlooked by the officers for several weeks; but last week things began to come to a head when two C.O.'s were put in the hole for refusing to fold their arms and the rest of us were threatened. Night before last about fifty of us, all men who are working, refused to fold our arms on command. They are trying to tighten up on the discipline here and are more than likely to make good their threat of putting us all in solitary confinement on bread and water.

For some strange reason I have felt happier since things have come to a head than in a long time past. I fear my conscience has been pricking me more than I realized. Were it not for the bedbugs, I should positively look forward to solitary and even as it is, I am not sure that I am not ready. The last few weeks have seen a sort of rebirth of my prayer life and I am beginning to long to have more time to think and pray. Solitary may be the best thing in the world for me; at any rate it holds no terrors for me. I think the administration is perplexed to know what to do with the C.O.'s. They want to keep them all separate from the other prisoners, I think, in order to enforce real military discipline here, but there are so many varieties of C.O.'s. There are those who will do absolutely nothing and those who will work but won't salute and still others who will work and salute but will buck in a minute should there be any tightening of the discipline. They are not here to be disciplined. And so it goes. Poor government! Why don't they let us go?

The time has gone fast since I last wrote you. There have been two or three interesting operations. I certainly should hate to leave this work. I guess no man in the prison has a better job.

Should I ever be placed in solitary, you will know that my letter privileges are greatly reduced, which will be one hardship. I think a man is allowed to receive mail and write once every two weeks but of this I am not certain. Visiting may be difficult or impossible. I am feeling fine and very happy, thanks partly to your letter of last night.

Memorial Day

I hasten to write you again this week in order that what I wrote you in my last letter may not cause you further worry. I am not being sent to the hole for the reason that after considerable explanation on the part of the authorities here, I believe I can continue to fold my arms for officers as heretofore. Since my last letter the following developments with regard to the matter have taken place.

On the day before yesterday I was sitting on the porch of the hospital by the front door when the dental surgeon and one of his assistants passed. Another fellow who was sitting next to me rose as they passed and folded his arms, and I sat tight. The fact that my bench-mate rose and I did not attracted the major's attention to me, and he turned back to see what was the matter. When I saw that he wanted to speak to me, I stood up but did not fold my arms. He wanted to know what was the trouble. I told him that I was a C.O. and not accustomed to folding my arms, whereupon he took my number. I somehow felt relieved that a matter which has been causing me considerable bother for some time had at last come to a head. I felt I was ready for the hole.

That night the assistant commandant visited the C.O. barracks in order to read the riot act to us as the authorities wish to prevent if possible a recurrence of the riot and shooting of a week or so ago. One of the provisions of the act read to us was that at the sounding of the mutiny bell or whistle, all prisoners not involved in the trouble should run with their hands over their heads to the open space in front of the barracks and there stand with their arms folded in order to show that they did not bear arms or weapons of any kind.

At the conclusion of the colonel's reading of the riot act, he undertook to explain the custom of folding arms, and in so doing he insisted that it was not in any way meant for a salute. His whole speech rather upset me and I was pretty much up in the air as to what course to pursue at my trial on the following day. With all of the colonel's explanation, I could not help feeling that the custom was a mark of respect to the uniform which I absolutely do not feel and hence ought not to give.

Yesterday as I expected, I was called to the executive office to appear before the major. He first questioned me concerning the circumstances attending my refusal and the reasons for my action. He then more or less repeated the colonel's explanation of folding arms. The interview ended by his asking me whether I wished to persist in my refusal to fold my arms or to continue the practice. I was not ready at the time to go to the hole on the issue and desiring more time in which to consider the matter, I said I would fold my arms. I don't think I would enjoy solitary very much unless my mind was easy on the cause of my being there, and at present that is not possible.

Today I feel more like continuing the practice but only on the conditions which have been explained to me. If at some future time I feel that the folding of arms is looked upon by the army as a sign of respect to its officers, I think I shall quit but for the present the matter has blown over.

All's well.

June 9

The biggest event since I last wrote was a visit from Kirby Page last Wednesday. I was busy helping with an operation in the morning and so was unable to see Kirby until one o'clock, but we had from then until six, part of the time with Fred also. It was a great treat. Kirby is such a wonderful spirit; he just brought new life to both Fred and me and we have felt better ever since.

A few days ago my name was struck off the parole check list so that I am no longer able to go out as heretofore for walks in the evening. I am not very sorry because most of the walks are so infested with mosquitoes that there is little pleasure in walking and besides I have been over them all again and again. The administration here is tightening up on everything, and all paroles not actually working outside the walls have been taken from the list.

I have been kept on much longer than I expected to be and I could only be put back now, if at all, as an act of special favor, and I do not care to be the object of special privilege.

I am enjoying life in the sixth cantonment very much. It is not at all like life in a prison. Every evening after count, we have a dance which lasts for about half an hour until lights go out. The music is furnished by a Gibson mandolin but it or rather its player makes good dance music. Fred is the finest dancer I ever met and he is teaching me. It is great sport and I am getting the waltz down pretty well now. So far I have taken the lady's part but tonight I tried the man's and got along pretty well. After the dance we take a shower and turn in. I have just had my shower and am finishing this letter before turning in. Tho I am not working at all hard these days, I seem to want to sleep all the time. I guess it is the reaction from a hard winter. It sure would be great to get home for a rest.

June 10

I have had practically nothing to do in the surgery ward all day. Things are letting up a bit in the hospital; in fact I may soon be out of a job as the places of prisoners are fast being filled by new medical corps men.

June 11

An acute appendicitis operation this morning kept me busy most of the day. Today a bunch of new corps men was assigned at the hospital and all but two prisoner-nurses were relieved from duty. I was retained in the operating room.

June 14

Thursday I lost my fine job at the hospital. I was booked, as I wrote you, to continue my work there but the night that the other men were released, some of them broke into the drug room and stole several gallons of alcohol, whisky, etc., and seemed generally to have had a celebration. It is not the first time such a thing has happened and when the captain heard of it, I guess he thought the only thing to do was to get rid of every prisoner working in the hospital. My, but it hurt to go! I have worked hard there for over seven months and I have given my very best. The corps man who took my place is eager to get out of the army; he hated like poison to come here, and for that reason I question whether he will put his heart into the work as I have. But such is the way of the army.

Friday morning the men relieved from the hospital were formed into a "sanitary detail" for the purpose of killing bedbugs in the wings. The captain paid me quite a compliment when he called me before the other men and especially recommended me to the lieutenant who was to take charge of the work. He seemed to regret the necessity of releasing me from the hospital. Friday we spent in the sub-basement of the large barracks for the purpose of filling clean straw ticks, but as we had only a few ticks we slept most of the time on the straw. This morning we worked harder lugging straw ticks to the top of the eighth tier of cells where a part of the detail went over the cells

with kerosene sprays. Everyone hates the work and is trying to get out of it.

Erling Lunde had his sentence cut to one year a couple
of days ago. I wonder if that may happen to me. If I get
my sentence cut to a year and do not lose good time, I shall
be out September 14th; that won't give me much summer
at home, will it?

June 24

Seventeen C.O.'s received immediate discharges yesterday. It may foreshadow the release of more of us soon. I
am being assigned to the poultry farm today.

July 1

Last Tuesday about three o'clock I packed all my prison
belongings into a blanket, tumbled it onto my back and
hiked about a mile and a half to the chicken ranch.

The chicken ranch is situated on the slope of a hill overlooking a sort of valley scattered all over with fields of
grain or corn separated here and there by strips or groves
of trees. There is no suggestion of a prison anywhere.
There are no bars on the long, low stone building which
the men occupy as their quarters. Civilians are in charge
of the work, and the one lone soldier is more a clerk than
a guard and rarely carries a gun. When he does, it is usually after some one has just reported a fox in the vicinity
of some chicken house.

Tuesday evening I had a real supper, the first since I
left the hospital. After supper, accompanied by one of my
old hospital friends, who is now room orderly and the rep-

[235]

resentative of the men here in their dealings with the authorities, I had a look at the new palatial quarters which are now nearly completed for the use of the paroles quartered on the ranch. We had a dandy shower bath in the new building and then strolled up to the lone soldier's house and listened to his phonograph as we lolled on the grass. Believe me, it was great, not the music for it was only ragtime, nor the phonograph for it must have been made before the flood, but just the whole idea. Do you folks who can go and come pretty much as you please, take in a movie now and then or hear a real concert, realize what a privilege is yours? There was no lining up for count, no officers, but about nine o'clock we all moved our bunks out of the building where we are supposed to sleep and put them in the road just out in front where we went to bed under the open sky. Oh my, it was great!

Wednesday morning after a breakfast of delicious oatmeal and *real* milk, bacon, two eggs and coffee, I went to work pitching straw out of one of the chicken houses. About ten-thirty I was summoned from my work, ordered to pack up all my things and report immediately to the executive officer. Needless to say I was at a complete loss to account for this turn of events, nor were my suspicions in the least aroused when the guard on a rather flimsy excuse accompanied me on my mile and a half hike back to the prison. He was armed with a revolver.

The first person I met on entering the walls was Fred who said that both of us had had our paroles recalled for reasons unknown and were to be quartered in the fourth wing basement and were to work on one of the gangs. He was just on his way up to the executive office, and I accompanied him. Nothing could have taken me more by surprise than my interview with the executive officer.

When Fred and I asked to be relieved from "Stray Shots,"[1] Fred as editor acted as spokesman and in fact saw the morale officer, under whom "Stray Shots" is edited, alone. He gave as our reasons for withdrawing, first, our desire for outside work, and second, a feeling that we could not edit "Stray Shots" as a magazine whose purpose was to build up military morale, etc., which both of us felt was the editorial policy which the colonel in charge was striving for. When I went before the executive officer, he stated that my parole had been revoked and read as his reason for doing so a note from the morale officer to the effect that because we could not agree with him in his editorial policy we ought to have our paroles taken from us. He then stated that men who were unwilling to help to make this prison a better place to live in had no right to a parole. You could pretty near have knocked me over with a feather. Upon my asking under what conditions I could regain my parole, the executive officer decided to look further into the matter and asked Fred and me to return after dinner. We did so but waited all afternoon without results.

Wednesday night Fred and I were put in the fourth wing basement with the other C.O.'s. It was a sweltering hot night. The windows in the basement are just high enough so that what little breeze there might have been floated well over the beds without touching them. Fortunately our bunks were not in the cells but in the corridor

[1] Gray had been assisting Leighton in the work on the prison paper.

just in front, but they were crowded close together. It was not long after lights went out before the bedbugs got busy. It is the vermin, not the guards or bars, which make a prison such a nightmare. To doze off after an exasperating struggle only to be awakened a few minutes later to tear madly at a foot or arm which has just been bitten and feel as if all the blood in your body is being pumped into it at high pressure, is a nightly experience of practically every prisoner in hot weather. Many, many times that night I got up and walked the floor, tired as I was. About two-thirty in the morning a thunderstorm sprang up and it cooled things down enough to permit of a few hours rest before early mess call.

Thursday we again returned to the executive office where after some waiting we were called to hear what the morale officer had to say to us. Practically his first remark was that he had nothing at all against me, but that reports had come to him from several sources that Fred had been arguing his position with several persons in the post and that his actions in so doing could be interpreted in no other light than propaganda. He said he had nothing against either of us and that he did not object to our keeping our paroles if we would not indulge in propaganda. I, for one, stated that I had never to my knowledge done any propaganda work either inside the prison or outside as a parole, and that I saw no reason why I could not agree to refrain from such propaganda so long as I chose to retain my parole. Fred also agreed to keep his lips sealed and our paroles were returned. That afternoon both of us moved out to the chicken ranch. Perhaps it may be said that we have been traitors to the cause of free speech but I do not believe so. What the authorities mean by propaganda is talk which would incite people against the government, and I do not believe in this. Furthermore, I am coming more and more to feel that when a man seeks to live his philosophy, talk is almost unnecessary.

Friday morning I was assigned as assistant to a civilian in charge of one of the chicken houses. We had some three thousand young chicks hardly a month old to look after. It was very interesting work. Yesterday, however, the civilian under whom I was working left, and this morning two new men took over the house. Today I have been doing odd jobs about the place. I shall probably continue as a sort of utility man until one of the prisoners in charge of a house goes out; I have been promised his place.

It is bedtime but it is still light enough to write as I sit here on my bed out in the road. It is a beautiful evening and a cool breeze is going to make it fine for sleeping. We are having great meals and it promises to be a splendid summer out here. God certainly made the world beautiful. I wonder why man should do so much to make it miserable for his fellows by depriving them of the right to enjoy it.

Love to all.

July 4

The last few days I have been pitching straw out of chicken houses and doing sundry other odd jobs. I am in tiptop health altho I am awfully soft when it comes to hard work. This life is going to be great for me and if I am released by fall, I ought to be in splendid condition for college.

Love to all.

On July 14 Prisoners 15175 and 16295 (Fred Leighton) sent the following communication to the executive officer on the subject of barracks paroles.

1. In interview with you on June 26th we accepted barracks parole work on the farm colony poultry farm and agreed to the condition that we should conduct no propaganda.

2. We hereby request release from that promise for the following reasons: Broadly interpreted it deprives us of the right even to answer questions pertaining to our religious beliefs and to our position as conscientious objectors. This promise abrogates our fundamental right of free speech. We have not in the past sought to force our opinions upon others nor do we intend to do so in the future. Yet we feel that voluntarily to relinquish the right to make known our beliefs as Christians is to deny the basic principles of justice and freedom and to deny the Master.

3. Furthermore, we desire to turn in our barracks paroles for the reasons set forth below: Altho both of us held barracks paroles for several months previous to coming outside the walls to work and to live, this experience on the

poultry farm where we have been so obviously our own guards, and also our recent consideration of the question as to whether we ought to accept a home parole have caused us to analyze more closely the nature of a barracks parole. We have come to the conclusion that the holding of a star parole implies a tacit admission on our part of the justice of our imprisonment. We feel this to be so because in promising not to escape we become sharers with the state in the responsibility for our being here. By force the state has, we feel, unjustly imprisoned us; it bears full responsibility for that act. By obligating ourselves not to escape we have assumed part of that responsibility. This we can no longer do. It is, we trust, needless to add that we have not in the past, nor do we in the present even remotely contemplate escape.

4. Having learned through experience that we have pursued a wrong course in this respect, we feel it incumbent upon us to follow the truth as we now see it.

5. We respectfully submit our requests for your consideration and await action at your discretion.

Before any action, however, could be taken upon this request, a change of situation rendered the action unnecessary. It was a Friday of July heat when orders came to the chicken ranch for Gray to return at once to the D.B. Upon his arrival he was confined in a sub-basement, two stories beneath the ground, a place in use for solitary confinement. Others, all of them C.O.'s but two, were similarly confined, similarly ignorant of the reason for this unusual treatment.

About three o'clock the following morning, Saturday, the men were aroused and ordered to gather their belongings, a simple operation since they consisted at best of blanket, toothbrush, comb, and Bible. Breakfast was hurriedly served, coffee and wieners, and the men were ordered to line up in front of their cells. Here they were handcuffed in pairs; two "hardened criminals" in the group were further secured with foot-shackles. With their blankets and baggage they were marched outside the barracks and taken to the railroad station.

Trifles have an aspect of comedy in a tragic setting. One of the prisoners was a Seventh-Day Adventist whose religion forbade him to work on Saturday, and for him, as for the Hebrew of old, to carry a burden was work. Accordingly he refused to carry his load. In disgust the officer tied it on his back, but the prisoner calmly slipped the knot and the bag and blanket fell to the ground. They would have been left behind and lost had not Gray and another man agreed between them to carry the additional luggage.

The early hour of their departure from the prison suggested extreme haste or secrecy; such may have been the purpose of those in charge when the little group left the post, but events proved the haste unneeded, for from four A.M. until noon the twenty-two men sat idle on a railroad siding.

After hours of waiting and uncertainty, the train arrived

which was to carry them on, "destination unknown." But in the minds of many of the men there was practical certainty. Rumor had it that all of the C.O.'s were to be segregated for the remainder of their sentences at Fort Douglas, an army post pleasantly located near Salt Lake City, Utah. Already there had been transfers of groups of C.O.'s from Leavenworth to Douglas, and the prospect was not disheartening.

Douglas, an army post which had been used as an internment camp for enemy aliens, had promise of a decency and a humanity of living which the three great military prisons, Fort Jay on Governor's Island, Fort Leavenworth, and Alcatraz in San Francisco Bay did not have. Stories of the horror of solitary confinement at Jay were common, and as for Alcatraz, to the military prisoner of 1918 the word was synonymous with living death. The tragedy of two of the three Hofer brothers had stamped Alcatraz in thousands of minds as an earthly hell.

The story has been previously told, first in a pamphlet issued by the American Industrial Company, and later by Norman Thomas in his study of the conscientious objector.

The three Hofer brothers were Hutterites, a religious sect holding many things in common with the Mennonites, and as such had been imprisoned for their refusal to fight. As a part of their faith they steadfastly refused to don any uniform. Moreover, it was their belief that their duty to God forbade their submitting to military command. Their refusal to obey orders soon brought them to Alcatraz where they were assigned to the dungeon.

CHARACTER "BAD"

Mr. Thomas tells the story in these graphic words:[1] "Alcatraz has a dungeon which is a place of horror. Moisture stands on the walls. It is so dark that a man cannot see his hand at arm's length, and according to prisoners who have been there, it is infested with rats. (This latter statement has been denied by the officers who claim that the rats were the creatures of the overwrought imagination of the prisoners.) . . .

"Beaten by guards (the chaplain is said to have struck one of them with his fists) they [the Hofer brothers] were sent down into the 'hole' as the dungeon is called. Their civilian clothing taken from them, clad only in their underwear, without covering of any kind, they were kept day and night in this wet, foul dungeon. During the day they were 'strung up'—that is, manacled in accordance with military regulations. Beside them on the floor were soldier uniforms and they were promised relief if they would put them on and agree to obey. Jacob Wipf [another protestant], afterwards said, 'We had decided that to wear the uniform was not what God would have us do. It was a question of doing our religious duty, not one of living or dying, and we never wore the uniform.'

"Under these conditions they continued for thirty-six hours practically without food and with too little water to drink. Finally the authorities could not continue their brutality, and the policy of stringing up the Huttrains was

[1] From *The Conscientious Objector in America* by Norman Thomas. Copyright 1923 by B. W. Huebsch, Inc. Published by The Viking Press, Inc., New York.

abandoned. They were kept in the hole, however, for five days with insufficient drinking water and no toilet facilities. Then they were released, and during the remainder of their stay at Alcatraz were treated fairly well. Their experience in the dungeon had weakened them so much, however, that when, some weeks later, they were transferred to the severe climate of Fort Leavenworth they felt the change keenly. In Leavenworth they refused to work and were consequently confined in solitary. Two of them contracted pneumonia and were taken to the hospital too late to save their lives. As an ironical climax to the tragedy, whether premeditated or unconscious, the body of one was sent home in a military uniform."

The death of these two men had occurred during the first week of Gray's assignment to the hospital at Leavenworth, and their gruesome story had made a deep impress on him and his fellow prisoners. To mention it was to call to mind Alcatraz and to hear the name was to shudder.

Meanwhile the group of prisoners was speeding west. The guard in charge had been a patient at the hospital during Gray's weeks of duty as orderly, and knowing something of his sense of responsibility, he chose him to assist with the work of kitchen police for the trip.

The trip to Salt Lake City would not be long, twenty-four hours perhaps. At La Junta the Santa Fé divides, one line going south, one going north. It would be the northern division that would take them to Salt Lake City and Douglas.

Kansas in mid-July burns with heat. The hills lie

parched; the grain immobile. La Junta is a junction town. The train sped on. Every man in the group was waiting to have his hope confirmed, his expectation made certain.

There was the crunch of engine wheels at a switch-crossing, the jar and vibration being felt thruout the train; then to the right instead of to the left the men saw the tracks—tracks leading to the north and Douglas. A solemn hush fell on the group. Every face was strained, every body held tense, nervously still. Some one whispered, "Alcatraz." There rose a mighty rumble of human spirits in despair, "Alcatraz! Alcatraz!"

But the Alcatraz of the Hofer brothers was not the Alcatraz Gray was to know.

Alcatraz, California
July 28

With such limited writing privileges as are extended to the prisoners here, I cannot begin to write the many, many things I have to tell so here's hoping I am out soon and can record them in a real letter home. Did you dream how your wish might sound in your letter of "Thursday evening" when you wrote "I hope you will be far away when this greeting reaches Leavenworth"? I surely am "far away" from Leavenworth; in fact about as far away as I could get and still stay within the bounds of the U.S.A. Alcatraz is a real prison, but I shall save writing about it till another day. It is far superior to Leavenworth, however, in almost every way. The food is excellent, with plenty of variety and lots of it; everything is scrupulously clean; the few "overseers" I have had dealings with have been exceedingly courteous, and it is great to see some of my old friends again. I am working in the carpenter shop where I think it is going to be pretty easy to pull time.[1] If I am released before fall and can come home by the Great Northern could you and Father meet me at Yellowstone Park?

August 3

I have just finished supper which consisted among other things of pineapple ice cream with chocolate sauce and delicious cocoanut frosted cake. The meals here are excellent and, the home board excepted, I have seldom fared better. Strange as it may seem considering the disappointment which I know my delayed release has brought to you, I am extraordinarily happy. A real prison isn't a half-bad place to live in. The silent system, or "iron rule" as it was referred to at Leavenworth, while by no means rigorously enforced here does confine us to our cells a good deal; we are required to spend all time there when not in the mess hall or at work, and this has enabled me to get some reading done once more. There is an excellent library here. Last week I read Hermann Sudermann's *Regina* and Winston Churchill's *The Crisis*. I fairly lived in a dream while reading the latter. What a thriller it is! Practically all day I have been reading Thomas Hardy's *Tess of the D'Urbervilles*. My work as a carpenter is very interesting and I am learning a lot. I am so happy I whistle at my work most all the time. Thursday was an especially

[1] To store up merits gained thru good behavior, which would serve to shorten the prison sentence.

red letter day because we had a splendid concert in the evening. No more news allowed for this week. Heaps of love to all.

August 10

Since no letter from home has put in an appearance this past week, I fear you have fallen a victim to your hunch about my release. Perhaps I am unduly pessimistic on that score but at least my pessimism protects me from any disappointment as I note the passing of the weeks and as yet no evidence of a "blue seal." If sharing my pessimism will induce you to write as if my release were not expected, I pray you be pessimistic for your letters to me mean more than I can ever tell. The past week has fairly flown by. For considerably over a week now I have been entrusted with doing the finishing woodwork on a new house, putting in window casings, doors, cupboards, stairs, etc., a most fascinating and instructive occupation at which the time passes almost unnoticed. The superior discipline existing here has made possible a much more orderly life than during the past months of my imprisonment, and I seem to have a fondness for orderliness. Perhaps it is only my imagination but I have felt as if God were nearer to me since I came here. I have had a better chance to get quiet and think and pray. As ever at such times I grow discontented with myself. I fall so far short of my ideal. I wish I were not so thoughtless and selfish especially about little things. If I were not, I know I could both give and receive so much more from my fellow prisoners. I fear I am far too self-centered. What a constant scrap it is to get the better of our selfish selves and what a discouraging one sometimes!

August 17

I think if the authorities here knew how genuinely I could sing the praises of Alcatraz to my friends, my letter writing privileges would be greatly extended for I sure am pleased with the place. I am strangely happy. Life never looked so bright, nor has time ever passed more rapidly. I love my work and it presents a real opportunity. Previous to coming here I question whether I should ever have had the self-confidence to apply for work as a skilled carpenter, but I think I could do that now. I have taken a real interest in my task and I guess the foremen have noticed it for I have been given the best job in a shop of thirty-three men as I wrote last week, doing the interior woodwork in a new house. I am practically my own boss receiving my orders direct from the civilian foreman in the morning instead of bit by bit from the soldier bosses. Only one other man has been helping me regularly.

Last night I finished Meredith's *The Egoist*, a really wonderful book, and today I have read the first hundred pages of William De Morgan's *Joseph Vance*. It certainly starts off well. I have made a list of books I want to read which will keep me going all winter if I am destined to stay here. The biggest event of the past week was Fred's arrival from Leavenworth on Tuesday. He went thru a lot after I left and he looks it with his head shaved and his cheeks pale and sunken. He has been in the hospital since Friday morning. I have heard nothing and am beginning to get anxious. It is over two weeks since I have heard from home. Please take my advice of last week seriously and don't bank on my homecoming no matter what Washington promises. Heaps of love to you all.

August 25

This morning I finished *Joseph Vance*. It takes almost an effort to remember that I am I and not Joseph Vance and that I have duties to perform, for seldom have I lived so completely in any book, even becoming vaguely identified with its hero in my dreams at night. If I could write like De Morgan, I should be strongly tempted to write an autobiography. I think there are experiences in my life quite as interesting as anything Joseph Vance experienced which would supply excellent material for a novel. But here I am as ever raving about myself as if nobody else in the world was of any interest to me. Fred was released from the hospital last Monday (only a bilious attack) but while I have gained him back, I lost during the past week a man who has become a real friend since we left Leavenworth, handcuffed together over five weeks ago; he left last Friday for his home in Georgia. He is one of the most gentle, lovable men I have ever known and some day he must be a guest in our home. What a rare little group of choice friends God has blessed me with during the past year! Certainly in that respect it has been a huge success and after all, is there anything greater a man could wish

[250]

for than friends in Christ, men with a great purpose to help usher in the Kingdom of God? I never was happier or in better health and need only a homecoming to make my joy complete.

On Sunday, September first, Gray wrote home as usual, little dreaming it would be his last "prison" letter.

September 1

The biggest event of the past week was yesterday when I was called in from work and found Max Chaplin awaiting me. There was delay in getting permission and we had only about half an hour together but oh! oh! how good it was just to see him. We rushed from one topic to another and I hardly remember now what we did talk about but it doesn't matter, it was so good just to see him.

I question whether my delayed release is all due to red tape. I think a release would surprise me much more than remaining here all winter—and then some.

My work the past week has been an especial source of joy; it was the making of a railing around a bedroom porch. The weather has been beautiful all week; the porch overlooked the bay with its many ships, the work in itself was interesting and then, best of all, there were some little girls who made friends with me. What a joy just to be near some little children after so many months with scarcely ever even the sight of a child.

This afternoon Fred and I had a good visit out in the

[251]

yard. Our work has separated us and I have not seen much of Fred lately. It was great in the yard this afternoon with the splendid view of the Golden Gate. We are superbly located for scenery and right opposite San Francisco. Four times a day as I go to and from my work I am able to view the old fair grounds. The Art Museum, California and Oregon Buildings, the tall monument and the great flag staff seem to be all that remain. Who could have guessed when we spent so many happy days there that four years later I would view the place as a prisoner on the rock opposite them? But in spite of that fact, I never was happier in my life and certainly never in better health.

On the day of the signing of the Armistice, Philip Gray had written President Wilson and Secretary Baker asking for clemency toward Harold. In the months that followed he left no stone unturned in his efforts to gain his son's freedom but the government mills grind slowly and not always with logic. As the letters suggest, there were numerous rumors of an early release and again and again hope was aroused only to be cast down.

It was not until late summer that the document with "the blue seal" reached Alcatraz. Under date of August 23, 1919, there is this communication:

In the case of General Prisoner Harold S. Gray, formerly private, Co. A, 1st Casual Battalion, Fort Riley, Kansas, now confined at the Pacific Branch, U. S. Disciplinary

CHARACTER "BAD"

Barracks, Alcatraz, California, the unexecuted portion of the sentence of confinement published in General Court-Martial Orders, No. 92, Camp Funston, Kansas, November 14, 1918, is, by direction of the President, remitted.

By order of the Secretary of War:

Signed by the Adjutant General

On September 4th the colonel in charge of Alcatraz telegraphed Mr. Gray:

"Your son Harold Gray will be released September fifth. He will be furnished with transportation to Detroit."

On the date promised, September 5, 1919, Gray crossed the bay from Alcatraz to the Golden Gate. In his pocket was carfare to Detroit and a dishonorable discharge, stating, "That Harold S. Gray, private 1st Battalion, Conscientious Objectors, National Army, is hereby dishonorably discharged from the military service of the United States." In that official document were listed the usual items of physical identification and health record, military qualifications, etc. Under Remarks there was written this single comment:

Character "Bad"

Harold Gray carried with him, however, vastly more than carfare and a dishonorable discharge; he carried with him the certainty of freedom, freedom of privacy which he had so sorely missed, freedom of action whereby he could reënter Harvard and prepare himself for the years

[253]

ahead, and still more precious, a new and larger portion of that freedom which in reality man had never been able to take from him during the months at Custer, Riley, Leavenworth, or Alcátraz, the freedom to serve his Master according to the wisdom of his own intellect and conscience.

>>>>>>>>>>>>>>>>>>>>><<<<<<<<<<<<<<<<<<<<

EPILOGUE

Detroit, Michigan
17 February 1934

IT WILL be fifteen years next September since I was handed my dishonorable discharge from the army, fifteen years since the great iron gates of Alcatraz swung open and I found myself once more a free man. Altho I have felt deeply on the problem of war, I have never conceived of my main mission in life as a campaigner against war.

Once out of prison, my first thought was to complete my college education at Harvard, where I obtained my A.B., and later my M.A., degree. The next four years I spent in China, as an instructor in economics at Central China University, Wuchang, six hundred miles up the Yangtse River.

A leave of absence in 1926 found me back in Cambridge, Massachusetts, engaged again in graduate work. I had planned to spend one year in additional study, but the unsettled conditions in China, due to the revolution, made necessary the extension of my leave for another year, and then the continued chaos and the responsibility for a growing family made the wisdom of returning at all seem exceedingly doubtful. Gradually and painfully the idea was weighed and considered and finally abandoned.

My study of economics had made me eager to supplement my theoretical training with practical experience. In the summer of 1928 I returned to Detroit and sought a job with one of the large trust companies, where I began to acquire some practical knowledge of the world of banking and finance.

My three years in banking, timed as they were to include the frenzied days of 1928-29 and the great collapse which followed, served only to focus my attention afresh on the problem of economic insecurity. In the spring of 1932, therefore, I set out to realize the long-cherished dream of establishing a community farm which might give to those connected with it a greater sense of economic security through a combination of agriculture and industry, to be supplemented later by democratic ownership and control. The working out of such an experiment has engaged my attention ever since.

Altho I have taken no active part in any of the many so-called peace organizations or movements during the past fifteen years or engaged in anti-war propaganda, this does not mean that I have outgrown any of the major convictions that finally landed me behind prison bars. Today if I were to rewrite my defense before the court-martial, I should probably phrase my position in somewhat different and perhaps more modern terms, but the convictions therein expressed remain essentially unchanged.

During the past fifteen years I have been painfully conscious at times of the difficulty of living up to even a few of the many logical implications of my stand, but if you were to ask me whether, under similar circumstances, I would again follow the same course of action, I should answer you unequivocally that I would. I still feel as deeply as ever that war and conscription are wrong and that I, as a Christian, cannot support or condone them.

On one or two occasions in the last few years I have been asked to speak on my experiences as a conscientious objector. On such occasions I have spoken less of the theological convictions which underlay my stand than of some of the antichristian and anti-social actions and attitudes which war engenders. I have stressed the first shock which I received at the immorality of London in war-time and a colleague's remark made during those days that he for one was prepared to turn the whole bally show over to Germany and apologize for its being in such rotten condition. I have stressed the public reaction in London to the German air raids and the unreasoning demands for reprisals: if the Germans kill our women and children, we must go and do likewise. I have stressed my shock on first entering a German prison camp to realize that the Germans were human like myself, as sincere and as conscientious in their belief that they were fighting a war of self-defense as any Ally, and how overpowered I was by the folly of seeking to settle men's differences by scientific butchery.

I have stressed how war sounds the death knell to truth and honesty, not so much thru the organized spread of deliberate falsehood as thru the suppression of so much that is essential to a balanced judgment. I have stressed how supreme in time of war is the law of military necessity, in the name of which men may be ordered to commit any crime or atrocity, to sacrifice the life and violate the personality of any man, woman, or child, and so to reverse the order of things as to condemn the virtues of kindness and mercy, generosity and love, and exalt in their place the vices of blind cruelty and hate.

Finally, I have stressed my belief that Christ faced the problem of war, that his rejection as the promised Messiah and his final crucifixion were due in no small part to his conviction that the method of violence and war was inconsistent with the kind of kingdom he had come to establish, and that to employ a method inconsistent with the end would lead to the ultimate defeat of the end itself. Altho it is these aspects of war upon which I have publicly laid emphasis, I still hold to the main theological tenets set forth in my court-martial defense.

I have a little son eight years old. There are times when I hope he may be spared certain of the experiences I have lived thru, but then again I am not so sure. Some one once said that what happens to us doesn't matter much and it doesn't matter for long, but how we react to what happens matters a great deal and it may matter forever. I do not ask that my son be spared the necessity of taking his stand on vital moral issues; I pray only that in all honesty he may seek to follow the highest light he can find. If some day he should take his stand against war and be persecuted for it, facing prison or even death, if need be, for his convictions, I shall harbor just a touch of inward pride and shall offer a prayer of thanksgiving for a son who is prepared to follow his conscience, come what may.

HAROLD STUDLEY GRAY